NURTURING
the Gifted
Female

To the spirits who encircle
and sustain me ~

Robert, my steadfast spirit;
David, my conscientious spirit;
and
Michael, my free spirit ~

I dedicate my work.

NURTURING
the Gifted
Female

A Guide for
Educators
and Parents

Joy L. Navan

Foreword by
Elizabeth A. Meckstroth

CORWIN PRESS
A SAGE Company

For information:

Corwin Press
A SAGE Company
2455 Teller Road
Thousand Oaks, California 91320
www.corwinpress.com

SAGE India Pvt. Ltd.
B 1/I 1 Mohan Cooperative
  Industrial Area
Mathura Road, New Delhi 110 044
India

SAGE Ltd.
1 Oliver's Yard
55 City Road
London, EC1Y 1SP
United Kingdom

SAGE Asia-Pacific Pte. Ltd.
33 Pekin Street #02-01
Far East Square
Singapore 048763

Printed in the United States of America

Library of Congress Cataloging-in-Publication Data

Navan, Joy L.
  Nurturing the gifted female : a guide for educators and parents / Joy L. Navan.
      p. cm.
  Includes bibliographical references and index.
  ISBN 978-1-4129-6136-3 (cloth : acid-free paper) — ISBN 978-1-4129-6137-0
(pbk. : acid-free paper)
  1. Gifted girls—Education. 2. Gifted girls—Psychology. 3. Parental influences.
4. Self-actualization (Psychology) I. Title.
  LC3993.2.N38 2009
  371.95082—dc22

                                                                  2008004870

This book is printed on acid-free paper.

07   08   09   10   11   10 9 8 7 6 5 4 3 2 1

Acquisitions Editor:	David Chao
Editorial Assistants:	Mary Dang
Production Editor:	Appingo Publishing Services
Cover Designer:	Karine Hovsepian
Graphic Designer:	Sandra Sauvajot

Contents

Foreword

I became Joy Navan's fan during her process of becoming certified in the Annemarie Roeper Method of Qualitative Assessment. The more I learned about her expansive life experiences, the greater I admired and enjoyed her. Joy has amassed multiple lifetimes of awareness into her vast experiences. Her global reference points expand her horizons and transition times and cultures.

I found the essence of this work in her first chapter: *This book is a product of the wisdom of the females in our lives—who teach us daily that their world is limitless when given the means to face their life experiences with confidence and zest. It is not a how-to manual. Rather, it is a journey of perceiving and understanding our daughters and how we—as the significant adults in their lives—can become collaborators in their mission* (p. 5). With Joy's sensitive, acute careful listening and extensive research, we are enriched and empowered to serve. Her insights and sensitivity reflect the decades she spent supporting gifted females across their lifespan. Her years of intimately nurturing gifted children, their parents, and various aged university students enliven the stories that will embrace your soul. From her own life experiences, Joy understands gifted females from tots to crones. You'll love becoming Joy's companion. She'll hold your hand, make you laugh, patiently guide you, step-by-step, to value your Self and your ability to support and nurture yourself and the developing women you encounter.

"I always felt invisible." During my decades of supporting gifted children and their families, their being invisible theme was woven into gifted women's stories. Rarity renders them inconceivable. Here, Joy inclusively embraces females' widely diverse, sometimes subtle gifts. Rather than imposing a gifted or non-gifted dichotomy based on academic status, Joy verifies sometimes immeasurable, subtle strengths and traits such as autonomy, musical affinity, resilience, nurturing others, visual acuity. . . ever honoring uniqueness, valuing

each girl/woman for her quirky passions, her own precious dreams. Joy identifies giftedness by inner core qualities that drive a gifted girl/woman, through her inner essence she brings into her world. With this perspective as a parent or a teacher, you can hold up a mirror of possibilities to the females who trust and beseech you.

In this book you hold volumes of information distilled to their essence. You'll fall in love with some children who sparkle and grin right on the page! You will resonate with females' spirit and minds as you experience aware, sensitive youngsters to wise older women. You'll emerge empowered by knowing what it takes for girls and women to thrive.

You will spend cozy time with Joy Navan, who sees beyond the obvious into intuiting more about what is going on in the inner lives of gifted girls and women. Her empathy delves into subtle, profound meanings and matters. Grounded in abundant research, Joy's compassion embraces females from the inside out: facts and feelings. Here you have supportive research and compelling life stories to affirm what gifted females want us to know about them. These are their realities, concerns and hopes of their parents and educators. Your time with Joy will render you intimately familiar with the girls and women portrayed in these chapters. You'll emerge empowered by knowing what it takes for girls and women to thrive.

You readers will likely sustain a paradigm shift in your acceptance and expectations of gifted females. You'll touch some depths and folds of your Self that had not been heard. You'll notice nuances of fear, passion, maybe repressed remorse or resentment. You selected a beautiful, wise mentor in Joy Navan. Her life story is about raising up people.

This volume is about you and how you perceive yourself and the girls and women you live with and encounter. You'll find yourself in these pages. You will glean insights into your own traits that might have been seen as pathological by others. You will redefine your tender sensitivity and focused concerns for others as generous compassion, rather than being "too sensitive." You will come to admire your varied passions and projects, even though many were only started and sampled, and more are still in their idea stages.

You teach what you are. If you were drawn to this book, you will likely glean insights about your Self. You may recognize yourself on these pages and evolve your self judgments. As many have, you may grieve that you and others did not acknowledge your profound sensitivities and ideas as assets and, through your reading you may enter a process of redefining your Self.

This book is about you and your expanded empathetic awareness that transforms our own expectations and responses to women. Information can only serve girls and women to the extent that we readers incorporate and reflect what we glean from these portraits. It is about you, particularly. You teach what you are. You can only give what you are to give. Any paradigm change you hope for can emerge from your single shift in what you expect from yourself and how you respect women of all ages.

Your personal windfall in this volume is that most of the many suggestions for nurturing young women and girls aptly apply to yourself, male or female! You'll be coached in self efficacy, finding your voice, affiliation, resilience. Welcome to the inner lives of bright girls and astute women portrayed by a very wise woman whose heart, mind, and spirit have nurtured a myriad of gifted females.

Blessings,
Elizabeth A. Meckstroth

Preface

It has been a pleasure to teach, collaborate, and mentor able girls and young women for over thirty-five years in the field of education. Through my qualitative research the voices of girls and women resounded with enthusiasm, telling of their hopes and anxieties, their beliefs and their dreams. The voices are from the Northeast, the South, the Midwest, and the West. They are American—including African American, Native American, Hispanic American and first generation American. They are from Pacific Rim nations and from Europe. They are from rural schools, village schools, private schools, urban schools and universities. They are our world and the purpose of this book is to tell their stories.

Through their voices we come to know girls and young women and how—though they represent different cultures and social strata—they share a need to develop universal constructs of success that will promote the healthy development of their gifts. We learn of their *resilience* and their *efficacy*, of how they develop their *autonomy* and at the same time value their *collaboration* with others. Through psychological frameworks, the reader will view the successful development of girls.

Within each chapter parents and educators learn valuable strategies that will assist the girls, their families, and their teachers to discover and strengthen students' gifts. This is a book about gifted girls, but it is also about girls whose gifts are yet to be discovered and nurtured. The lessons of the girls in this book apply to females and males; for we all have the need to grow and nurture Self. Likewise, the educational interventions presented are best educational practices for all students, not just our gifted girls. However, gifted students, because of their keen intellectual abilities, are developmentally ready for certain interventions earlier in their educational careers than the general population.

The case studies that begin each chapter present specific aspects of women's development in such a way that the reader observes constructive, psychological traits as they appear in high ability girls. Thus, the reader sees a picture of how certain strengths reveal themselves and how they benefit the healthy development of the individual. Within each chapter are strategies for parents, teachers and counselors. Each chapter ends with a reflective exercise that applies the material to professional practice.

Chapter 1 begins with a case study narrative, which is a tapestry of voices from several students. The narrative introduces important issues in raising gifted daughters. Strengths and concerns include a thirst for learning at a young age, early mastery of skills, multiple talents, the need for parent advocacy and mentors, a strong sense of justice and fairness, and the risk of social isolation.

Giftedness reveals itself not only through the individual's intellectual potential and cognitive characteristics. Rather, gifted children differ emotionally both in depth and intensity of their feelings. Chapter 2 explores giftedness using a lens that is grounded in the psychological construct of *Self*. It presents psychological and emotional characteristics of giftedness, explores the concept of *overexcitabilities* as observed in gifted children and how they present themselves in the gifted female, and describes an assessment method which is achieving notable success in understanding the world of the gifted child. Chapter 3 presents an overview of gifted girls and their developmental needs, and investigates the cognitive, behavioral and environmental factors of women's development.

Each of Chapters 4 through 9 examines important psychological constructs that are key to a young woman's progress toward wholeness. Additionally, each chapter offers parental and educational interventions to assist the young female in her development. Chapter 4 explores the importance of *voice*, calling on the work of Jean Baker Miller and Carolyn Gilligan, among others. Chapter 5 traces the development of *resilience* through the stories of versatility and coping of gifted young women. In Chapter 6 we explore how our daughters find themselves and their strengths through *affiliation*, and then withdraw to their sacred space to reflect and to discover their *autonomy*. For our girls (and all learners) a core construct in their success as learners is their perception of efficacy. In Chapter 7, we explore the construct of *self-efficacy* and detail ways that parents, educators and the community can assist students in strengthening their belief in themselves and their abilities.

Having successfully cultivated and nurtured the previous constructs, the gifted girl experiences the emergence of *agency*—a sense of herself as a significant participant in a society that needs her gifts. Chapter 8 explores the construct of self-agency and demonstrates ways in which gifted young women tap into and apply personal agency. An overwhelming sense of ethical grounding and a celebration of being female were vital tones that pervaded all of the research. In Chapter 9 a case study introduces Lydia, who explains that she and other gifted girls need to celebrate the sensitivities, the emotions and the ethical grounding that are integral to the female spirit. The final chapter presents an annotated list of resources—books, programs, and educational materials that will be helpful to educators, parents and gifted girls.

Acknowledgments

The journey toward this book was one of illumination and joy. The diverse voices of all the gifted girls and women I have known resonate throughout. The selfless sharing of their hopes, dreams, and concerns wrote each line. To them I am enormously grateful. I acknowledge with appreciation as well the valuable contributions to our knowledge of women's development of researchers who created a body of literature that is a well-spring of my own growth. In particular, the works of Jean Baker Miller, Mary Belenky and her colleagues, and Carol Gilligan provided a new lens through which we gain clarity and insight. In the area of the gifted female, I thank all the researchers who have given our discipline a new awareness of the distinct characteristics and needs of gifted girls. In particular, I will always be grateful to the mentoring and friendship of Janice Leroux. She taught me to perceive the gifted woman with all her healthy and positive strengths; not with a deficit model of barriers and difficulties. Finally, to Annemarie Roeper—who has educated me both indirectly and directly for over three decades, who affirms my vision for the gifted, and who released in me the view of the *Self of giftedness*—I express my deepest admiration and gratitude.

It has been a pleasure to work with my editors at Corwin Press—Allyson Sharp and David Chao and their assistant, Mary Dang. They have supported me throughout the review and publishing process. Their professionalism as well as personal attention improved this book immeasurably. Finally, thanks to Belinda Thresher at Appingo Publishing Services. Her attention and support were invaluable in making this book a reality.

About the Author

**Joy L. Navan** directs the Center for Gifted Studies at Murray State University in Kentucky, where she serves as an associate professor and program director for the graduate endorsement program in Gifted and Talented Education. The program is offered in the traditional classroom setting and online, in both English and Spanish. Dr. Navan is a Certified Practitioner of the Annemarie Roeper Method of Qualitative Assessment®, and performs assessments in English and Spanish. She earned her Ph.D. from the University of Ottawa, Canada, where she studied under Janice Leroux and assisted her in researching the lives of eminent women.

A teacher for 27 years, Dr. Navan spent many of them working with gifted students at the secondary level. During that time, she also served as an adjunct instructor at St. Lawrence University, where she taught a course in the methods of teaching second languages and supervised student teachers. With almost four decades in the field of education, she has developed curriculum and monographs for gifted and general education and published numerous scholarly articles nationally and internationally. Fluent in Spanish, she initiated and directs an exchange program with gifted American and Spanish students and currently coordinates an online gifted and talented certificate program in Spanish. She served on the Kentucky Advisory Council for Gifted and Talented Education, is a member and past board member of the Kentucky Association for Gifted Education and serves on the board of the Kentucky Odyssey of the Mind. She is a member of the National Association for Gifted Children and the World Council for Gifted and Talented Children. Dr. Navan is an active member of Phi Delta Kappa International, an honorary association of professional educators.

1

Introduction
Gifted Voices

Threads in the Tapestry

Cameron

When Cameron was five, having mastered addition and subtraction, she begun learning multiplication in the back seat of her parents' car while on vacation. Her parents were already aware of the many special qualities of their only child, but this event became a touchstone for them in their quest to provide the necessary resources for their highly able child to be challenged to her potential. Questions flooded their minds. How capable was their daughter? Where were her particular strengths? What were her emotional needs? How could schools respond to her individual characteristics?

Caroline

The first time I met Caroline was when she was five. She took me out to the garden of her house, giving me long explanations of the different flowers, butterflies, and other living things found in the garden. She was delighted to share all of this with a visitor, dancing from one part of the garden to the other and connecting different phenomena to favorite childhood stories, songs, and family memories. Nature was her element, and this became even more apparent as she made comparisons between this environment and the land surrounding her parents' cottage at the lake, telling me of the frogs, snakes, and other creatures she had seen.

Jordyn

Throughout her childhood Jordyn was recognized for her sense of justice and her leadership. While other children ignored the Hispanic girl in the class who could communicate in English only a little, Jordyn became her playground pal and invited her for sleepovers and stayed at her friend's house in turn. As a seven-year-old, Jordyn established her own craft business to pay the expenses for the family's vacation to a famous theme park, a goal that she met in two years.

Katie

Even after being accelerated into another grade, Katie ran for class office among unfamiliar peers. Because she grew and changed so rapidly in both intellectual and psychosocial ways, her parents and the gifted-child specialist that worked with them soon realized that they needed to make a commitment to flexibility to assist in her healthy development. Through the years Katie skipped several grades, yet she continued to be a wholesome, well-rounded, and well-adjusted young girl. Her mission was to help humanity through medical research.

Cameron

Middle school was a difficult time for Cameron. She longed to fit in—to be popular in the group—and was tempted to go underground, to hide her superb abilities from her peers. Thanks to supportive parents and due to her own belief in herself, she chose instead to be true to her potential and continue her journey as a highly gifted student. The consequences of her choice required her to draw on her personal strengths as she endured teasing and derision not just from her classmates, but also from teachers who failed to understand how their joking criticism of her high motivation and abilities hurt a child whose giftedness was marked by heightened awareness and sensitivity to unfairness. Thus, although she found these experiences hurtful, Cameron learned to develop a variety of healthy coping strategies and consequently she emerged as a more resilient individual.

Elyssa

In her late adolescent years, Elyssa found that she had exhausted the resources available to her in high school and chose to enroll in an early entrance program at a university renowned for its science and engineering programs. Observing her in this environment, one saw that her actions and perspectives demonstrated her strong understanding of herself and her abilities, a self-perception that pervaded all aspects of her life. She believed that she had not yet explored the limits of her capabilities, and with hard work she could accomplish any goal that she set for herself. Her behavior in a challenging academic setting, where she was almost two years younger than the other first-year college students in her classes, manifested her self-perceptions and her abilities.

Laykesha

In a college biology class, Laykesha, an African-American student much younger than the other first-year students in the course, organized her text, notes, and other resources accessibly on her desk. She prepared text notes from her reading the night before that included vocabulary and terms that she referred to during the class. As the professor lectured, she took notes and carefully drew diagrams and models in her notebook, referring from time to time to her text or text notes. She not only volunteered often in the university classroom, but was often the focus of higher-level questioning by her professor.

Anna

Anna, whose first language was Lithuanian, was highly verbal and also keenly capable with social skills, which she balanced with academic responsibilities. Anna's Lithuanian name means "grace," and she believed that the female aspect of her Self was what allowed her to be fully human—not just her capabilities as a biologist or engineer. Outside of the classroom, as a member of student organizations and in sports, she connected, nurtured, and communicated effectively. As a leader, she was collaborative and drew others into decision making and problem solving.

Vanessa

An important part of Vanessa's day was time spent with her mentor. She loved painting and was working with a professional artist who guided her in planning and painting a mural in the commons area, where all in the academy could enjoy her gift. Vanessa and her mentor discussed the project enthusiastically, as equals, using artistic terms freely as together they coaxed from her creativity the conceptualization of the work in progress. She was lost in the bliss of the creative process, as an autonomous practicing professional. She entered what Csikszenmihalyi (1990) identified as "flow," in which one is highly engaged in a task to the point that it is so gratifying that it holds the individual's total attention and motivation.

Weaving the Stories

Giftedness is a greater awareness, a greater sensitivity, and a greater ability to understand and transform perceptions into intellectual and emotional experiences.

—ANNEMARIE ROEPER

The preceding descriptions represent a number of gifted females whom I had the pleasure of teaching and mentoring throughout my professional life. I weave these memories with knowledge of human development to illustrate that most of the gifted girls and young women who enrich our lives and who contribute to understanding our gifted daughters share similar characteristics—characteristics that support their healthy development and the fulfillment of their potential. Although each is a unique individual, they have developed and used common psychological strengths and behaviors to overcome difficulties. They grow into vigorous young women who impact the wellbeing of their surroundings through their positive contributions. As a result, many of them are already valued members of our society as counselors, physical therapists, social workers, engineers, architects, medical researchers, and in other professions that enhance and improve humankind.

The glimpses above display many facets of giftedness that we may find in gifted students. Some of the themes and indicators are listed below. A caution to the reader is the reality that recognizing and identifying the gifted is not as simple as checking off characteristics from a list. We will explore these as well as other gifted characteristics in the voices of successful gifted girls throughout the book.

Facets of Giftedness

- High potential in one or more academic areas
- Keen awareness of the interconnectedness of the natural world
- The joy of creative activity
- A strong sense of justice and leadership
- A deep empathy for others
- A belief in one's responsibility to improve Self and the world
- The difficult early adolescent passage and the risk of losing voice
- A powerful resilience and versatile coping abilities
- Belief in one's abilities
- Superior self-regulated learning skills
- An awareness of one's strengths as a female
- The importance in working with a mentor
- The benefits of being a practicing professional

Using the stories of gifted females who thrive, we can understand some of the facets of our own daughters, nieces, and granddaughters. Additionally, through understanding and applying appropriate educational strategies, we can serve in roles of support and guidance as they weave their own threads of giftedness, motivation, and potential, creating a rich tapestry that allows them to develop full and healthy lives. This book is a product of the wisdom of the females in our lives, who teach us daily that their world is limitless when given the means to face their life experiences with confidence and zest. It is not a how-to manual. Rather, it is a journey of perceiving and understanding our daughters and how we—as the significant adults in their lives—can become collaborators in their mission.

Reflective Research in the Classroom

1. Look at the characteristics of gifted children listed in **Facets of Giftedness.**

2. Use the list to reflect on the traits of students in your classroom. Pay particular attention to your female students.

3. Jot down the names of students who display three or more of these characteristics.

4. Based on this reflection, what are your next steps in terms of:

- Recommendations for the gifted program at your school?

- Response to the needs of the students whom you have noticed display gifted attributes?

2

Giftedness:
A Qualitative Difference

Lilly's Voice

Lilly, a five-year-old, walks into her family's living room and takes her place at the piano as if she has entered a fine European concert hall and seated herself at the greatest grand piano imaginable. She places her hands over the keys, assumes an illustrative pose, and begins to play. I notice that she has no sheet music and does not look at either hand, yet she plays a lovely classical melody with superb musical expression. Her eyes acquire a dreamy look, and she smiles with pleasure as she continues to evoke a melancholic mood through her performance.

"What is the name of that piece?" I ask as she finishes. "It does not have a name yet," she replies. Later, her parents explain that it is a piece that Lilly composed and that she is preparing for a recital. I murmur, "A five-year-old composing?" "Yes," answer her parents with the same tone of amazement, "she is."

Lilly shows me her room and plays a recording of Tchaikovsky's "Dance of the Sugar Plum Fairy." Dancing with leaps and pirouettes, she accompanies the music perfectly, expressing poses that reflect the changing tones and intensity of the music. Once again, Lilly is totally engaged, lost in her performance as if transported to the stage. The music ends, and she curtsies gracefully.

The Passions of Giftedness

Lilly is an exceptionally gifted five-year-old who exhibits the intense sensitivities that parents and others often observe in gifted children of her advanced abilities. She reacts readily—and at times with heightened intensity—to stimuli in her environment. She exhibits imaginative playfulness as a strong visual thinker and creative daydreamer. Emotional giftedness manifests itself in her artistic passions, strong emotions, and in the pure joy she exhibits when playing or performing. Lilly displays many qualities that gifted experts in educating gifted children recognize as indicators of high levels of giftedness. Observable characteristics, grounded in the psychological concept of *Self*, tell us much about the emotional and imaginational world of the gifted child. Examining traits of giftedness through this lens can reveal its many dimensions—intellectual, emotional, social, and intuitive. Furthermore, understanding emotional giftedness and the strong sensitivities that accompany it is key to our insight into the world of the gifted female.

Intellectual Characteristics

When we encounter gifted children, we are principally aware of their *astute intellectual abilities*. The intellectually gifted child is driven to understand and thrives when involved in finding original solutions to complex problems. The child continually wants to know all about things he or she encounters in the world. Able to multitask and jump from activity to activity, the child also can sit and ponder for long periods of time. Because they leap through cognitive developmental stages and notice details that others of their age peers do not, gifted children are often self-taught, having achieved abstract reasoning ability much earlier. This reasoning skill allows them to intuitively solve problems, think in symbols, and make logical projections.

Another aspect of intellectual giftedness in some children is their strong need for precision and order. They sometimes learn to tell time at an early age and express the intense need to strictly schedule their time and to neatly organize their belongings. The need to order their world is understandable when we realize that the gifted brain is so busy thinking and making constant connections that it may be difficult to maintain a sense of balance. Having a feeling of control over the environment is a way of coping with the varied stimuli in their environment.

Intellectual Traits of Giftedness

- Thirst for learning
- Delights in problem solving
- Strong intellectual curiosity
- Grasps meaning quickly
- Loves to ponder over certain topics
- Early abstract reasoning
- Intuitive problem solver
- Keen logical thinking

Note: Gifted children may display some or all of these characteristics.

Emotional Traits

A second characteristic that keen observers notice when interacting with gifted individuals is their sensitivity, which is evident both emotionally and morally. The most apparent characteristic of emotionally gifted children is their passion. I think of the musical and expressive intonations in the voices of some young gifted girls with whom I have interacted. When they are excited, their exuberance has an intensity that draws you into their enthusiasm. The sadness in their voices when they speak of a tragedy—real or imagined—touches you as well.

Many gifted children have powerful emotional imaginations from an early age. Creatively gifted children often have an imaginary friend or treat pets as special friends. Because they are early abstract thinkers, imaginative scenarios in daydreams or dreams seem quite real to our young gifted, but they may not have the emotional maturity to process them. They may be extremely attached to and have difficulty separating from their mothers. Often they will express intense fears of the dark, of sleep, or of nightmares. A seven-year-old child that I assessed talked about how she was fine in her room at night until the last track of her classical CD began to play. Then she had to go to her "little" bed, which was a small toddler's bed in the hallway outside her parents' bedroom. A number of families I have worked with report that they maintain a "family bed" because their young child is unable to sleep alone.

Emotional Aspects of Giftedness

- Passionate about certain themes
- Emotionally expressive
- Intensely imaginative
- Deeply empathetic
- Early sense of justice
- Socially naïve
- Fierce emotional attachment to one or both parents.

Note: Gifted children may display some or all of these characteristics.

Gifted children, and gifted girls in particular, are highly empathetic when siblings or friends are sad or hurt, and even very young gifted children worry about global problems like hunger, war, terrorism, or weather disasters. Some feel physical pain themselves when a relative, friend, or pet is injured. They also have a strong sense of justice that is evident from a young age. Socially, our gifted children are often naïve and may not recognize when they are being teased or even bullied. A father of a preschooler, for example, describes how an older child at school had his son, Jack, in a headlock and was squeezing his neck, causing him to begin to choke, when a teacher came upon them. Jack protested that the other boy was not being bad, that he was only teasing. Some of these traits of emotional giftedness also indicate a phenomenon of giftedness called *emotional overexcitability*. It is helpful to our understanding, if we explore what is meant by this term and how gifted children demonstrate other overexcitabilities.

Overexcitabilities

Lilly's parents recounted how they were aware that their daughter was "different" from birth. She had a difficult time sleeping, crying incessantly and inconsolably, if put in her crib alone. They also noticed that she was highly reactive to any stimulus in the environment—needing soft textures, soft light, soft sounds—in essence, requiring a very calm and peaceful environment. I noticed that, after a few seconds of playing the CD at what was a normal volume, she said it was too loud and turned it down. The lights in her room have pink lampshades and radiate a soft, rosy glow in the room, which is decorated in different shades of pink. As she showed me her tutus, she remarked that one of them had "scratchy sleeves," and she doesn't wear it. Although highly communicative, Lilly seems to remain on guard, protecting herself from too much intensity.

A mother of a child I worked with is concerned because her five-year-old daughter has "meltdowns" every evening—dissolving in tears and sobs for no apparent reason. The teacher of a first grader recommends that the parents make plans to have their child evaluated for Asperger syndrome because he insists on precision and following procedures to the letter. Another child continues to tell the story of a wounded butterfly and wonders about its fate years after observing it struggle to fly with a broken wing. Several parents find that their children need quieting rituals at bedtime, and many need white noise, soft music, or nature recordings to fall asleep at night. These examples illustrate some of the overexcitabilities I have observed in gifted children. Contrary to the fears of their parents, there is no pathology to be diagnosed in these cases. Rather, their intellectual and emotional giftedness often manifests itself through their overexcitabilities.

Types of Overexcitabilities

- Psychomotor
- Sensual
- Intellectual
- Imaginational
- Emotional

Note: Gifted children may display some or all of these characteristics.

The concept of overexcitabilities provides an explanation for why certain individuals react strongly to stimuli in their environment. All of us receive input from our environment through our senses, but we somehow are able to filter the messages in such a way that they do not overwhelm us intellectually, emotionally, or sensually. Dabrowski (1972) identified five areas in which the response to everyday events and natural occurrences for some individuals—especially for the gifted—is more intense, vivid, and longer-lasting. The reactions are both physical, involving the central nervous system, and psychological. These five areas of overexcitabilities include Psychomotor, Sensual, Intellectual, Imaginational, and Emotional (Lind, 2001). Intellectual overexcitability, which is recognized most easily by educators, parents, and other adults, expresses itself in the child's love of learning and her delight in problem solving, both mental and visual. Lilly, at five, constructs 500-piece jigsaw puzzles from the center outward. A young boy makes games of complex math problems, which he solves in his head without pencil or paper. And he very graciously chirps, "Correct!" when I manage to solve an equation he poses to me.

Gifted children have all or some of the five forms of overexcitability. Often, the more highly gifted the child is, the greater his or her intensity will be. Many experts in giftedness believe that the phenomenon of overexcitabilities is a key characteristic of gifted children and can be used as a tool to identify them. Unfortunately, all too often educators may view such traits—which are beyond the norm—as pathological, and a child may be misdiagnosed with attention deficit hyperactivity disorder (ADHD), autism, Asperger syndrome, or other disorders (Webb, Amend, Webb, Goerss, Beljan, & Olenchak, 2005).

Dabrowski believed that *emotional* overexcitability is core and that the other overexcitabilities emerge from the individual's emotional center. Children with this overexcitability will feel intense emotions and may show strong empathy for others or for animals. Often the child will experience so much emotion in the course of a day that she will have a "crying jag" in the late afternoon or after supper. With their heightened sensitivity, relationships are crucial to those with emotional overexcitability, but for the same reason, false, shallow friendships are meaningless to them, and they may have just one or two lifelong friends.

Psychomotor overexcitability manifests itself as the need for a lot of movement and restlessness. During assessment sessions, several students I have examined carried on focused, intricate conversations, solved mental problems and riddles, or narrated their own stories while simultaneously moving around the room, looking out the window, or doodling with pencil and paper. Many of them talk very fast, and their words are accompanied by lots of gestures, theatrical facial expressions, and an emotional tone of voice. Having spent much time in many test-driven schools, I know of many teachers who consider unsolicited movement and multitasking during lessons to be unacceptable, yet gifted children who have psychomotor overexcitability cannot do otherwise. Their *Self*—their perception of who they are— contrasts drastically with the lock-step behaviors that are the norm in classrooms where teachers feel pressured to produce test results. Moreover, the fact that these children can remain focused and accomplish tasks at a level significantly beyond their peers while at the same time needing movement is an indication that they do not necessarily suffer from ADHD.

Parents often report to me that their children need soft fabrics or struggle against wearing socks because the seams bother them, and parents often must remove the tags from clothing because they irritate the child. Parents tell me as well how their children cannot eat certain foods because certain textures choke them or that certain smells provoke intense and often socially uncomfortable reactions. These are characteristics of *sensual* overexcitability. Children also may react with panic at loud sounds and are highly sensitive to other types of stimuli, such as strong sunlight, wind, or the feel of leaves or grass against their skin. Sensual overexcitability is also the trait that moves them to dissolve in tears over viewing a work of art or hearing a piece of music, as did Mateo, a brilliant pianist, at three years old, upon hearing Pergolessi's *Stabat Mater* (the lovely, haunting theme in the movie *It's a Beautiful Life*). Lilly was transfixed when she saw ballet for the first time at two and insisted incessantly that she should take lessons until her parents finally relented. Her ballet teachers confirm that she has the gift of dance. A gifted woman I know cannot see a beautiful sunset without having the physical sensation that the light and colors are filling and sustaining her spirit.

Imaginational overexcitabilities reveal themselves in children who remember their dreams vividly and are prone to nightmares that are experienced with events, colors, and sounds so vibrant that the child may have a difficult time recognizing that they are not real. Those who love reading may think of their favorite characters as close friends and talk about them as if they are actual people that inhabit their everyday world. Children with this overexcitability are also quite creative, since they can easily perceive objects in different ways. If the parent or educator is not willing to accept such flexible ways of seeing, criticizing or refusing to recognize what the child sees differently, it can be devastating to her and cause her to doubt herself and her abilities. It will be easier to understand imaginational overexcitability for those readers who remember the comic strip in which the highly imaginative Calvin was often light-years away from the classroom fighting aliens with Hobbes, his tiger companion, while everyone else around him was solving simple math problems at their desks. I have my adult son's cherished collection of *Calvin and Hobbes* books by cartoonist Bill Watterson in my office and often share them with gifted students, who read them with relish, can easily identify with creatively mischievous Calvin, and usually know a highly rational adult who sees things just like Hobbes, the stuffed tiger!

Although students may display some of these traits and not be gifted, we find through research and observation that gifted students, especially the highly gifted, show most or all of them. It is sometimes difficult to distinguish between overexcitabilities and a sensory-motor integration problem. There is much current research in how to diagnose and distinguish them. Parents may want to seek out the help of a researcher with strong experience in both of these areas (Webb, et al., 2005).

Responding to Overexcitabilities

Psychomotor

Need for activity and movement: Provide the child with the opportunity to stretch and move about the room. Give her a soft ball to squeeze at her desk to relieve tension. Learning activities that provide for psychomotor involvement are appropriate.

Sleep needs: Develop a quieting nighttime ritual like reading a favorite storybook or sitting with the child as she falls asleep. Put a sleep machine or play quiet music in the child's room to help with falling asleep or to soothe her if the child wakes up during the night.

Sensual

Textures: Follow the child's lead by addressing the need for soft textures, removing tags from clothing, dressing her with seamless socks, and other, similar needs.

Foods: Respect the child's inability to tolerate certain tastes or the textures of some foods. Introduce them when the child seems better able to tolerate them.

Other stimuli in the environment: Be aware of strong reactions to odors, bright lights, sunlight, and loud noises. Adjust the environment to accommodate these sensitivities.

Intellectual

Need for mental challenge: Provide the child with the opportunity to learn and play strategy games and puzzles like chess and tangrams, riddles, and brain stretchers.

Need to make continuous progress in learning: Pre-assess the child's learning prior to instruction to ensure that she does not already know the material. Allow the student to progress at her own pace if she masters material at a faster rate than her peers.

Imaginational

Need to distinguish fantasy from reality: If the child has vivid nightmares and avoids sleep because of them, respect her feelings. Explain that while we sleep, the mind creates stories; some are funny while others are not. Tell her you understand how frightened she must feel. Assure the child that she is safe and that when she has bad dreams, her parents are there to comfort her.

Need to express creativity: In the classroom and at home provide for creativity and dramatic play—art materials, costumes, props, musical instruments, and writing paper. Encourage the child to express her vivid imagination through creative production.

Emotional

Intensity of emotions: Honor the child's feelings by acknowledging and helping, but not forcing, the child to verbalize them if appropriate. A child may want to talk about why she feels so sad or afraid, but not necessarily at the moment. Give the message that you are there, if and when she wants to talk.

Relationships: Gifted children are often socially naïve. If a child displays strong emotional overexcitabilities, help the child reflect on what friendship is and what friends do for one another. Discuss the qualities of a good friend. This will help the child create an "inner reflective rubric" that can help her be a good friend to others and recognize sincerity in others.

Lilly demonstrates many characteristics of a gifted child with overexcitabilities. In her need to connect emotionally with her teachers, her strong empathy for animals, and her compassion for all, she shows emotional overexcitability. She has strong psychomotor characteristics and needs a familiar ritual in the evenings to quiet her mind in order to fall asleep. She constantly is processing everything in her environment, and I observe the intensity with which she solves intricate jigsaw puzzles from the inside out. Sensually, she demonstrates intense sensitivity to fabrics, smells, tastes, and heightened aesthetic awareness. A loud and overstimulating preschool environment overwhelmed her keen sensibilities. She needs a peaceful educational environment in which educators are aware of her overexcitabilities.

Who Is This Child?

An excellent way to perceive, identify and attend to a child's giftedness is through a qualitative assessment process. The Annemarie Roeper Qualitative Assessment Method® (QA), developed and implemented by Dr. Roeper as a way of assessing children for her school, is a process that provides us with a view of the whole child in terms of emotional and intellectual giftedness.

While the emphasis in education of gifted children used to be on intellectual development alone, experts in the field are increasingly aware of the need to see the entire *self* of the gifted child and respond to *who* the child is (not only *what* the child is), if we are to promote healthy, self-actualizing growth. The QA method is *qualitative.* Rather than relying on a quantitative IQ test that discloses only the intellectual dimension of giftedness, QA looks at all facets of a child to reveal several aspects of giftedness—intellectual, emotional, overexcitabilities, and more.

The assessment process entails gathering information from a number of sources. We begin with a written narrative from the parents that represents the story of their child's development from birth and other relevant family background information. They are asked to highlight areas of significance in the child's development or behaviors, which would include developmental milestones, abilities, interests, and other qualitative information about their son or daughter. This is the assessor's first glimpse of the child and who she is.

The purpose of the narrative is two-fold. First, the certified practitioner gathers vital information about the development of the child. Second—and just as important—the practitioner is able to recognize what the perceptions of the parents are toward the child and toward the child's giftedness. For example, a father wrote a narrative about his highly gifted child in which he described his realization that the child was exceptionally able when his child was four years old. The father wrote about the guilt that he felt for not seeing the child's ability earlier, expressing his fear he had been a bad parent for not attending to the student's potential earlier!

Qualitative Assessment provides a window into the Soul of the child.
—LINDA SILVERMAN

Following the narrative, the QA practitioner meets with the parents in order to gather more information about the child and to develop a trusting, collaborative relationship with the parents so that both the parents and the practitioner can work together to reveal the child's self and understand how to respond to who she is. With this understanding, the practitioner then meets with the child. There is no specific plan or procedure to be followed in the session with the child; the child herself is the only agenda. The assessor merely allows the child to disclose her many features while they play a game, read together, or just talk. Sometimes the child plays in silence. Even in silence, the qualified practitioner gathers valuable information about the child and his or her gifts. This phase of the process is crucial, and thus the assessor brings a multitude of skills—observation and understanding of how giftedness reveals itself verbally, nonverbally and psychologically.

The child comes to the interview with many questions, such as: Am I safe? Is what I am going to say to be treated with respect? Is this person going to understand the depths of my feelings? Through the building and development of a trusting relationship with the child in the interview, the assessor becomes keenly aware of when the child invites the assessor to see facets of self, and when he or she must retreat until the child feels safe enough to share further revelations. The assessor realizes that he or she is invited into a deeper connection with the child and therefore must honor the collaboration that comes from the relationship. Finally, it is the assessor's specific task to discover the inner agenda of the child, the Self, the Soul. The assessor must genuinely and specifically reflect those facets not through directing the child, but rather by reflecting the child.

Qualitative Assessment Process

- Glimpse the Child—Parent Narrative
- Perceive the Child—Parent Interview
- Honor the Child—Child Interview
- Reveal the Child—Final Parent Session

Conclusion

To deny the Self of the child in all its facets—intellectual, emotional, sensitivities and intensities—is to deny who the gifted child is, to shut the child down. As Roeper and Higgins (2007) wisely explain, the Self is the center of each of us and from it radiates our emotions and motivation. It is through acknowledging that the gifted child's Self encompasses all facets of the individual that responsive adults can open the pathway to the child's authentic development. With the knowledge of how the child's giftedness is revealed, parents and others can create environments that honor the child and that allow the child to continue to thrive.

Spending time with Lilly and other emotionally gifted children is a pleasurable experience. One senses a glow of natural goodness and an early spiritual awareness of the wonder of the universe. These are joyful children, free spirits, and they are intensely committed to their own creative and intellectual development. It is fascinating and fulfilling to see them grow to feel comfortable with their environment while maintaining a rich, imaginational and creative play world as well.

Reflective Research in the Classroom

1. Look at the emotional characteristics of giftedness as shown on page 10.

2. Are there students in your classroom who demonstrate any of these qualities?

3. Choose one of the students that you identified in Step 2.

4. Prepare a case study of this child, looking for other indicators of giftedness.

5. Based on your findings, what modifications will you make in your classroom and instruction to meet the needs of this child?

3

The Gifted Female

Meg's Voice

A parent of gifted children was chatting with me at a soccer game one Saturday morning. She was concerned about her daughter, who was a new participant in their school's gifted program. She explained that Meg's two older brothers had been a part of the program for some years now. When the family was informed that their third child met the program requirements, she was a little surprised. It seems that while the boys were quite clever in math and sciences, Meg neither cared for nor excelled in those areas. She loved socializing, forming clubs with her friends, and organizing them into groups to perform services at school. She was also an avid reader, and her mother told me that at the beginning of 3rd grade, she was reading and comprehending books on the 7th grade level. The mother understood that these abilities qualified her to receive enrichment in Leadership and Language Arts.

"And why the concern?" I asked.

"She's just so different than the boys," said the mother. "While the boys are transparent in their strengths and accomplishments and not afraid to show them, I fear that Meg will be dropped from the program because she is

so reserved and unwilling to show what she knows. She's much more con-
cerned about children in Africa and ending wars than she is about compet-
ing with others in the program for the few opportunities that are available."
   I could see that Meg's mother and I had much to talk about.

Historical Overview

Capable young women of the early twenty-first century require a
repertoire of skills in light of the tensions of changing social and
career environments. They are heiresses to a history of underachievement among many able women who preceded them. Our students
come from distinct cultures and social backgrounds; they represent
socioeconomic groups from poverty to affluence, and widely differing
family constellations. However, research that follows the development of gifted people over several decades yields valuable information regarding common factors in the development of success. One
such study addresses several hundred gifted men and women, and
both groups reported that important predictors of their successful
adjustment as adults were family harmony, parents' educational
level, and the child's intellectual determination. Even with these
factors present, gender differences appeared in individual achievement both educationally and professionally. The relationship between
education and occupational success was twice as strong for men as
for women. For example, males with a Masters in Business
Administration may have become Presidents and CEOs of corpora-
tions, yet their female counterparts achieved leadership positions
much more rarely (Strip, Swassing, & Kidder, 1991).

   A study of past graduates of a private northeastern college sur-
veyed students from the early twentieth century through the 1980s
(Walker & Mehr, 1992). The authors found that the vast majority of
the gifted women felt that they failed to realize their potential. This
was the case despite their attendance at a school where a key mission
was to provide an educational setting where highly capable girls
learn and achieve to their potential. In general, women who had
entered careers followed the socially ascribed model of service occu-
pations. Almost half became teachers and 28 percent were social
workers, while only 5 percent entered medicine and engineering,
respectively. Surprisingly, the authors found no significant change in
these findings over the decades.

   The conversation with Meg's mother displays a fundamental reason why many of our gifted women fail to achieve their potential. The gifted female is still at risk of not being identified and not receiving services in gifted programs. This is especially true in underrepresented gifted populations—girls of color, of lower socioeconomic status, or with limited English proficiency. There are a multitude of other factors that determine either success or underachievement of gifted girls. Self-perception of their ability and self-confidence may decline over the course of their scholastic careers, and they may disguise their abilities and feelings. Rather than believing that they are highly able learners, many girls who I have instructed or advised express that their success is due to luck (Garrison, 1993; Reis & Callahan, 1996).

There are also significant differences between male and female adolescent perceptions of goals and their ability to achieve certain careers. Whereas gifted boys in one study were more definite about future career plans, girls considered plans that combined career and family. Most revealing in research (Reis, Callahan & Goldsmith, 1994) are indications that, even though three quarters of the gifted girls planned to work after having children, a majority of the boys thought that girls should stop working after children were born!

Such findings are distressing. Reflecting on the need of the gifted female to develop through relationships as well as to set high academic and career goals, we realize that those very relationships put her at risk of not developing her potential gifts. In addition, some gifted female students may be at high risk of developing depressive disorders. This is especially true for gifted students of color or from socioeconomically depressed areas. If they are not identified as gifted or are not supported in their gifts, these girls can feel isolated and helpless (Adams, 1996; Lovecky, 1996; Sands & Howard-Hamilton, 1995). By adolescence, today's highly able girls may be at risk of having developed several barriers to success as displayed below.

Barriers to Success

- Fear of success
- Lack of assertiveness
- Lowered academic and career expectations
- Failure to attribute success to ability
- Fragile sense of self-agency—necessary for choice and self-destiny

Characteristics of Highly Able Females

An essential factor in developing the gifted child's potential is for adults to understand gifted children's cognitive and emotional needs. Parents and teachers are the gifted child's best advocates, and this is especially true for girls, since they are often overlooked and may not be included in a school's gifted population. Additionally, girls tend to drop out of gifted programs at a higher rate than boys. It is important that girls who are gifted receive early identification of their potential. The opportunity to learn and interact at least some of the time with gifted peers is vital. Peers experience similar intellectual and emotional needs, and a teacher familiar with gifted children's needs can facilitate their self-understanding. Meg's school did a fine job in recognizing and identifying her abilities. Nevertheless, in order for her parents and teachers to be effective collaborators in planning services for their daughter, it is fundamental that parents and teachers alike understand the nature and needs of the gifted female.

What are notable characteristics of highly able girls that parents and educators need to understand? Themes that emerge in the literature regarding gifted young women as learners are displayed below.

The Gifted Female: Significant Findings

- The importance of early career education
- The vital influence of parents, educators, mentors, and role models
- The risk of underachievement
- The need to assist in their affective and emotional development

Characteristics of Success

There are particular characteristics that contribute to the success of gifted women. Kerr (1994) identified common factors shared by historically eminent women. Her findings include:

- Time alone
- A feeling of being different or special
- A sense of separateness
- Taking responsibility for oneself
- Refusal to acknowledge the limitations of gender

Additionally, the women found unique ways to integrate their diverse roles and to follow their passions (Kerr, 1994). Leroux (1994) identified three common threads among highly able university women and eminent women. These were the pressure to conform to social expectations; a spiral, connected path toward success; and recognition of the value of female collaborative relationships.

Research makes evident the need for parents and educators to understand and treat gifted girls in a manner that recognizes and enhances their learning and emotional development. Girls, as do all children, learn early on that they are capable and valued when they grow up in environments in which caring adults honor their potential and offer close, collaborative relationships. Educators who recognize and address similar needs in the classroom reinforce that the emotional and intellectual needs of gifted girls are indeed valid.

Educational Needs

High career expectations are clear indicators of a firm belief in one's ability. Parents and educators could ask themselves the following questions: Are there ways that gifted female students are being assisted in developing positive perceptions and abilities? Are they given the opportunity to ponder the importance of their career and personal decisions in a supportive, caring environment? An effective curriculum that contributes to the career success of highly able girls would include effective counseling, career exploration, and leadership training.

It is crucial that the gifted female adolescent have the opportunity to shadow successful females in different professional environments. Anna wrote in an early college entrance program, "Everyone—even gifted women, men, children—encounters times and situations when they do need support and to feel they are valuable. We all . . . need mentors or people who care for us to guide us despite our inclinations of independence."

When a gifted girl has determined what careers might interest her, educators can arrange a mentoring experience that will allow her to explore her potential career. For example, a school district in our university's region contacted me about an early adolescent who was accelerated in math and was interested in a career in Animal Sciences. She needed enrichment experiences beyond what her middle school could offer. A university student, herself a gifted young woman, agreed to mentor this girl. Since the young girl lived about an hour from campus, it was not viable for her to visit campus on a regular basis. Therefore, we were able to arrange an interactive long distance mentoring experience via instructional television in which mentor and student made regular contact and worked on projects together. Toward the end of the school year, the young girl was able to visit campus and tour the university and farm facilities and attend some classes. The benefits of designing programs that address the career needs of gifted girls are readily seen. They increase perceptions of efficacy, raise their goals, and support their accomplishments. Readers can only imagine the possibilities of arranging high quality, effective mentoring experiences with all the distance technology now available to educators and families.

Types of Mentoring Needs

- **Classroom Mentoring:** Kindergarten through 5th Grade
- **Active Mentoring:** Middle and High School Students
- **Distance Mentoring:** Middle and High School Students

Educational Interventions

Meg . . . is much more concerned about children in Africa and ending wars than she is about competing with others.

—MEG'S MOTHER

Family and educational interventions that will strengthen the gifted female's self-perceptions and provide a clear and purposeful vision of her future Self require early identification. For instance, if a gifted child enters kindergarten as an early reader or performing simple math operations and her teachers do not recognize her abilities, the child may not be identified for gifted services until third or fourth grade. As a result, the child is at risk of not making continuous progress in her learning for four or five years of schooling. The child is also in jeopardy of doubting herself and her abilities and losing motivation. What a tragedy it is to see the gifted reader endure letter-of-the-week activities ("A" is for Apple) when she could be reading two or more grade levels above her peers! Many parents complain to me in distress in this regard, and it is a common occurrence in many school districts across the nation. The expectation that all five-year-olds will be on the same, prescribed level is not feasible, given what we know about differences in individual development. Schools that embrace this belief close their eyes to the range of educational levels of children in the authentic classroom of the 21st century. We need effective gifted programs, but most importantly, we need effective *teachers*—in urban and rural schools, in all types of diverse communities—who are willing to *read the child*, and respond appropriately.

Another vital intervention that concerned adults can offer is to facilitate supportive relationships with other highly able females of all ages. Chapter 4 explores the importance of voice in the successful development of our able female learners. Voice is developed in relationship with others who share like abilities and sensitivities. Opportunities to interact with successful women give gifted girls positive role models who exemplify coping, leadership and communication skills. Relationships with counselors who understand the social and emotional needs of the gifted female are also essential to their development.

Developing a Mentoring Experience

1. Identify a student in the classroom who has enrichment needs that are beyond the current available resources.

2. Do a strengths/needs assessment of the student, looking at academic areas of strength, self-regulation skills (e.g., organization and goal setting), and strong interests.

3. Based on the assessment of strengths and needs, decide on the mentoring needs of your student.

4. Choose the type of mentoring that is appropriate (Classroom, Active, or Distance).

5. Search out an appropriate mentor in your community or beyond and:

    • Contact the professional to determine his or her willingness to be a mentor.

    • Brief the mentor on the goals and procedures for the experience.

        • Regular contact.

        • Opportunities to engage in problem-solving related to the mentor's profession.

- If distance mentoring, follow guidelines for appropriate use of technology in the school district. This will ensure the security of all participants.

6. Introduce the mentor to the student and provide them with an overview of the goals and procedures for the experience.

7. Monitor and modify the process as needed, asking for regular, written updates from the mentor and the student.

8. At the completion of the mentorship, perform an evaluation in order to document the growth and learning of the student.

Gifted children need the chance to follow their interests to intensity. Independent investigations, research, and authentic problem solving are examples of interventions that will address their needs. As with mentoring, early and sustained career exploration that includes shadowing high-achieving women is an excellent accommodation. Implementation of these interventions and strategies will result in higher self-perceptions and stronger self-belief.

Reflective Research in the Classroom

1. Look at the list of Barriers to Success on page 21.

2. Use the list to reflect on gifted females in your classroom.

3. Are there any who are at risk of successful development due to any of the listed barriers?

4. Based on this reflection, what can you do to assist your student by using some of the suggested interventions?

4

Voice

Hailey's Story

Hailey discovered words the first time her mother read nursery rhymes and other poetry to her. She imagined herself playing with the words—tossing them up in the air and watching them spiral, leap, and dance. Her favorite line early on was, "with up so floating many bells down" (Cummings, 1994). She invented special gestures to accompany the delightful sounds of her special words and shared them with all she met.

One day, she realized that she had the same magic as her mother since, suddenly, the shapes on the page began to speak to her, and she could give them voice by saying them out loud. This discovery left her breathless with excitement. She knew, although she could not explain it even to herself, that this was a powerful gift and that somehow her life was very different as a result of this magic. Years later, she remembered reading to her parents for the first time and seeing her parents smile at her, and at each other, as she read The Swing by Robert Louis Stevenson. Even when she stumbled over the strange word, "pleasantest," her mother took Hailey's finger and sounded it out for her as they traced the word together.

The day that Hailey began kindergarten, she was so proud! Along with her pencil box filled with lovely pencils and crayons, she took her favorite *book of poems to read to her teacher. Miss Betty was very busy that day, but Hailey was sure that next day she would want to hear her special words. Yet, it was early spring before Miss Betty realized that her intense and imaginative student could read. By that time, Hailey no longer carried a book with her to school each day. Miss Betty thought that her reading ability was confined to the sight words on display around the room.*

Something exciting did happen during kindergarten despite many other disappointments. About the third week—as the class was talking about the letter of the week, "C"—Hailey realized that she could use the letters that she had mastered long before kindergarten to make her own words. So, while Miss Betty was having the class repeat the sounds of "C," "D," and other letters, Hailey wrote poems under her desk that she took home to read to her little brother and that her mom put on the fridge with beautiful flower magnets. When her daddy came home from work, she would rush to the kitchen, snatch the papers, and read them to her father while they sat together in the big chair. Her parents continued to nourish her learning at home and wondered when her school would become aware of her abilities.

The school years came and went without much excitement. Most days, Hailey rushed home to explore the woods behind her house with the magnifying glass that her grandfather gave her for her birthday. She even enlisted the help of the neighbors to clean and protect the creek that ran behind several properties. After dinner, Hailey would dash to her room and choose a new book to read from the stack she had checked out at the village library the previous Saturday. Sunday afternoons were most special, because she could read two whole books instead of the one she read each night on weekdays. Her reading selections varied. She loved The Chronicles of Narnia, *poetry by Shel Silverstein, biographies, and anything about the natural world or other cultures. Words continued to be her very best friends, yet she loved to share them with anyone she knew.*

When she was in the fourth grade, Hailey encountered a different kind of words. After answering the science questions in class one day in a lesson that dealt with the same type of insects she had discovered and researched two summers before, Jimmy and Brad called her a "smarty pants" and said she needed to lose them. Hailey was deeply hurt and felt threatened in a way that she could not yet explain. It wasn't long before most of the kids frequently made hurtful remarks about her abilities and her love of learning. Hailey began to say less and less in class, and her teacher, Mrs. C., became frustrated with her lack of participation. It seemed that the girl she had thought of as her bright, shining star pupil was not so intelligent after all, and that it would not be a good idea to turn in the form she had completed recommending her for the school's enrichment program.

Divergence

Hailey has reached a time in her life when the reality of her world and her ideals diverge. For her and for other gifted girls like her, it is important for her parents and other adults in her life to be aware of this critical stage. Does she speak to significant adults, her peers, and friends sharing her love of words, nature, math, or other academics? Does she give voice to her emotions, her joy, and her fears? Or, does she sacrifice the truth of her own potential to preserve friendships and other relationships; choosing not to stand out in a classroom where few or no other students demonstrate the motivation to learn that she has? For Hailey and many other bright, motivated girls and young women, this is a crucial juncture in their development. They must either take the risk of being true to themselves and their gifts, or they must go underground, quieting their voice and their previously unbridled spirit in order to fit into a school environment that puts a lesser value on excellence for the sake of achieving minimum proficiency in all students. Hailey is at risk of losing her own unique voice, a voice that is vital to her intellectual and emotional development.

An overview of research regarding women's psychological development is helpful to our understanding of the importance of voice in the lives of gifted girls and all females. In her essential work, *Toward a New Psychology of Women*, Miller (1986) explained that through most of human history, women were defined at birth as members of a subordinate group. Therefore, our social and cultural histories have been shaped predominantly through males. In doing so, a male-dominated culture assigned to women tasks that are actually society's most vital needs—caring for family and others. Consequently, it is predominantly women who cultivate the emotions and passion for nurturing human development.

Women as nurturers have the opportunity to develop keen emotional, communication, and collaboration skills. The medium they use for refining these skills is voice. Hailey's voice, as with so many gifted females, shows the promise of significantly impacting her world. Girls need the autonomy to develop their voices in order to empower themselves and others. Miller explained that, because of empathic concern for others, women can achieve an understanding of their own empathy and transform it into the highest of human obligations—serving society. In recognizing and acknowledging their own voices, girls develop the strength to participate in the growth and creative transformation of others. This results in the formation of a dynamic and creative vision of personhood.

Miller also wrote that the ability to respond to others need not detract from sense of Self. One's identity validates itself through relationships. Society's recognition of the value of the connected Self would open the possibility of new and richer ways of living and functioning beings. Leadership and management styles that emphasize consensus-building, shared decision making, and other collaborative styles demonstrate the accuracy of Miller's thinking.

Carol Gilligan (1982) continued and built upon the work of Miller in her studies on the moral choices of women. She studied the responses of women confronted with decisions that required them to examine their values. Her research demonstrated how women, through their caring and connectedness with others, exhibit a high moral sense of human responsibility. She affirmed that women's moral essence is caring and easing the difficulties of others. Hailey, for example, is discovering her need to care through her concern for the natural environment.

In a study of adolescent girls in a private, all-female, preparatory school environment, Gilligan and colleagues affirmed that the primary way that female adolescents learn about Self is through relationships. It is through friendships with others—where through voice and affiliation they came to know themselves as well as others—that these young women were able to identify and explore barriers to their understanding of Self. Without these communicative relationships, girls withdraw into silence. With other girls like themselves, they find that they can acknowledge and vent their legitimate feelings in trusting relationships (Gilligan, Lyons, & Hanmer, 1990).

Brown and Gilligan (1992) traced the loss of voice during adolescence by girls who feel the pressure to conform to socially defined roles. During this time of disconnection—they are connected neither to girlhood, nor womanhood, nor to their own voice—they lose touch with their earlier, authentic selves as they are pressured to adopt a socially determined pattern of what it is to be a woman. Rather than confront the society that overwhelms them with expectations for "selflessness," they are silenced. The theme of Brown and Gilligan's book, reflected in its title—*Meeting at the Crossroads*—suggests that through healthy, connected relationships between women and girls, both benefit.

Gilligan (1994) explained that girls are at risk of withdrawing in silence from the very relationships that nurture them so as not to endanger the relationship with authentic feelings and words. In almost identical terms and during the same time frame, Miller (1994) arrived at the same conclusion, stating that adolescent girls hide a large part of their authentic Self in order to have relationships with others. Hailey's parents observe this in their daughter as she pulls herself away from academic achievement in an attempt to fit in with her classmates.

Pipher (1994) wrote of how adolescent girls struggle in their efforts to be both feminine and competent young adults. The adolescent girls in her study were conflicted with the split between socially learned behaviors—passivity, dependence, and lack of logic versus their own self-impetus to actualize as active, autonomous adults. She reported that as the girls in her research approach adolescence, they lose their resilience, become overly focused on body image, and may show a decline in achievement. Risk-taking and general optimism decline. Unfortunately, for all too many of Pipher's clients, their struggle led to a variety of psychological disorders.

Women become acutely aware of disconnection, false voices, and lack of authentic relationships in their adult world. Girls benefit from the connection with women who have made the journey through silence to voice and connectedness and wish to facilitate the journeys of others. Educators need to explore ways that different contexts provide the gifted female with the opportunity to develop healthy, connected relationships with peers and adults.

Developing Voice

Returning to Hailey, whose representative case study began this chapter, what are ways that parents and educators can assist in the development of her own unique voice? Girls need to hear the message that they are not "weird" or at fault for the way others react to their abilities and successes. I remember one gifted fifth grade student who would stop by my office once or twice a week at the beginning of her school year on the pretense of having a question about enrichment program activities. Our conversations would inevitably get around to her feelings of isolation in the regular classroom, where she was teased and ignored because her peers had no idea how to respond to her highly creative ideas. We arranged periodic conferences with her classroom teacher in order for the student to express her emotions and needs. These conversations helped the teacher to develop activities that would allow the student's intuitive and creative abilities to find an outlet. Structuring a time during the week for her to work with other highly imaginative students as a community of learners was another effective intervention.

Connected Teaching and Learning

All my learning and activities, the way I think, the things that I create, the things that I do, are all just forms of my interaction with others, with the people who I value and who value me.

—VANESSA

These words of a gifted young woman frame the need for educators to design instruction that enables girls to interact in a supportive environment with professors and with their peers. How can we create a learning community, an environment that permits learners to construct knowledge through shared inquiry? Connected Teaching (Belenky, Clinchy, Goldberger, & Tarule, 1986) is a model that promotes active communication and collaboration among learners and instructors. In a more traditional model of instruction, educators "deposit" knowledge and students struggle to look at that knowledge through the eyes of the professor. The result is that the learner—perceived by the educator as the *receiver* of information—may have little or no understanding of the depth and complexity of the content. Such a model does not allow for interaction with the material and with other learners, an important process in the learning cycle.

Constructivist learning differs from the traditional perspective by acknowledging that the individual learner must build knowledge, based on her prior knowledge and personal experience. The learner uses her unique cognitive ability and learning style, and her posture toward the material, to interact with new experience and store it in cognitive structures that are unique from those of any other learner (Sprinthall, Sprinthall, & Oja, 1998). Blending elements of constructivist learning with principles of Connected Teaching, teachers can facilitate the development of community. The following are examples of ways that educators can incorporate Connected Teaching and learning in the classroom.

Incorporating Personal Individual Experience

Because students need to absorb new information by integrating it into previously learned material, allow time during class for students to reflect and write about what they are learning. Ask them to do a *quick write* paragraph that addresses questions like the following: How does the new material help them understand the content of the course? How does it help them to shape major concepts that are the framework of the subject? Through the use of reflective journals, students examine new concepts in light of their personal framework and construct ways to apply fresh knowledge. Additionally, students might be given the opportunity to react to reflections of their peers, incorporating into their own understanding the experience of others.

Nurturing Each Other's Thoughts to Maturity through Consensus

Discussion that centers on the exploration of open-ended questions that provoke students to analyze, justify, and evaluate their thinking prompts the learner to refine and organize higher level thinking. Combining this style of questioning with the Socratic method of coaxing thought to maturity allows learners to nurture thoughts and build consensus. Withholding judgment as students think, reflect and discuss ideas in a non-critical environment promotes trust- and consensus-building.

Basing Teacher's Authority on Cooperation, Not Subordination

Imagine the classroom where learners acknowledge and act on basic democratic principles, such as tolerance, equity, and fairness. The teacher who recognizes and honors this style of classroom interaction will emphasize individual autonomy *and* the need for interdependence. The effective teacher helps students build collaborative cohorts, groups of like peers who value shared expertise, who promote both individual and group goals, and who enable the development of higher quality products.

A teacher who wants to group gifted and highly able students together and maximize students' collaboration might consider the Navan Collaborative Learning Model (Navan, 1994). In Figure 4.1 we see four important dynamics at play that do not necessarily occur in a basic cooperative grouping strategy. Classroom teachers can implement a collaborative learning group by addressing each of the components of the model.

Figure 4.1   The Navan Collaborative Learning Model

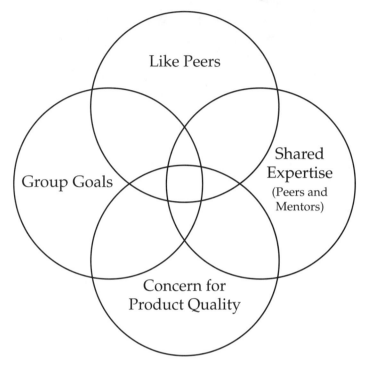

The first component is *Like Peers*, which indicates students who not only are highly able learners, but also share strengths and interests in the content of the activity. Second, each student draws on his or her particular interest and individual goals to negotiate a set of *Group Goals* that each student agrees are reflective of the needs of all. It would be very effective to allow students to create their own assessment, such as a rubric, at this time.

Due to both their ability in the chosen task and their interests, they enter the third phase of collaboration, *Shared Expertise*. Each student shares whatever resources necessary to accomplish their goals. These can include their own knowledge and skills, a variety of media resources, and mentors and other experts in the field. Out of each of the first three facets of collaboration, which have created a community of inquiry in which each student is empowered and enabled to pursue a personal interest to intensity, comes *Concern for Product Quality*. They collaborate with each other in the manner that practicing professionals would convene a group of colleagues to examine a problem, develop goals for a project, share their expertise, and create a quality product that addresses the identified need.

Midwife Model of Education

Educators who create communities of inquiry are believers in the midwife paradigm of education (Belenky, et al., 1986). Drawing on the work of Paulo Freire (1971), Belenky and colleagues concur that, rather than perceiving oneself as the depositor of knowledge, the connected teacher promotes individual and group problem solving. Students give birth to their own constructed knowledge, reflect on it, share it with others in a collaborative setting, and search for creative ways to incorporate new learning into future experiences.

Connected teaching and learning promotes group and self-efficacy and directly influences achievement and goal setting. As one gifted young woman stated while reflecting on her opportunity to learn in a unique secondary environment that promoted connected teaching and learning, "I think more people in society could work collectively like we have done in this school. We've built our own little community, we've built our own family, we've built up friendships that will last a lifetime "

Reflective Reading and Writing

Reading stories and books that feature bright young girls who experience similar challenges and feelings is another intervention that parents or educators can use with the gifted girl who is struggling to preserve her own unique voice. For example, in the series known as the *Time Quartet* by Madeleine L'Engle, heroine Meg Murry uses her intellect and her skills as a communicator to assist her family in a number of intergalactic adventures. An interesting note is that the gift that the author bestowed on Meg was the gift of kything, a telepathic form of communication. Gifted girls learn problem solving and communications skills as they identify with characters like themselves who become their early role models. Chapter 10 provides a list of further reading suggestions.

Encouraging girls to keep a journal is another way in which adults can assist gifted females in hearing and strengthening their inner voices. The personal journal becomes a reflective medium for the young girl to explore her thoughts, feelings, ideas and alternate voices. As she writes and reflects on her experiences, she is empowered to make individual choices concerning her world and her future. In the journal she can express her anger, doubts, joy, confusion—the whole range of emotions she experiences—at a time when she is uncertain if she can verbalize them socially. Journaling also gives her a space where she explores the many options that her abilities offer her future. Through writing about the many possibilities for her life, she tries them on like party dresses and considers which she likes and why they fit her unique being.

A Writers Circle

We should urge gifted female students to pursue creative writing through their journaling as well. They try out different voices in the exploration of several genres. One of my favorite enrichment activities was *The Writers Circle*, a day-long celebration of writing for gifted girls that I offered to schools and advocacy organizations. At the beginning of the day each girl received a pretty, fabric-covered journal that had a personal note that a teacher or I wrote to her inside the front cover. The message reflected some of the special aspects of the student and our wishes that the day become a special time of discovery of how she could use her journal to explore herself and the world. The day was structured into mini-workshops, each focusing on a particular genre of writing. The personal narrative—in which they wrote in depth about a favorite place where they felt peaceful and most themselves—was the breakthrough piece for some, where they found and explored their voice. For others, it was poetry—a pantoum, perhaps, or a chant. And some found new insight into their beliefs and their sentiments in the short story or a nature-writing piece. Each workshop always ended with everyone sitting in a circle and passing a long white satin ribbon from one to another as they shared their feelings and learning from the day. As the ribbon encircled the group and came back to the beginning, where it was tied to form one continuous circle, the girls listened to music and a poem about a circle of friends, always connected through their voices.

Planning a Writers Circle

- Choose a grade or a combination of grades you want to serve. Fourth and fifth grades are ideal.
- Invite local women authors to work with the girls for a day.

- Reserve a space that allows for both large and small group sessions.
- Send invitations to the gifted girls in those grades in your school with sign-up information.
- Based on those students who plan to attend, assign a group of girls to each author.
- Brief the authors on the students' abilities and suggestions for activities.
- Give each author a pretty journal for each girl and one for herself. The author will write a personalized note to each girl in front of the journal, welcoming her to *The Writers Circle*.
- Create an agenda that includes an opening, sessions with authors, breaks, lunch, and a closing.
- Plan lunch and purchase supplies.
- Celebrate writing!

Note: This would be a great activity for a parent group to plan and host as well.

A powerful element in *The Writers Circle* was that it provided time for the girls to collaborate and communicate with *like peers*, a term educators of the gifted use when describing grouping options that give gifted students the chance to study and collaborate with other students who share similar interests and abilities. Research shows that gifted children achieve better in educational environments where they have the chance to study and interact with others like themselves. Furthermore, if a teacher has a class of 25 or more students with a range of abilities and needs, the one or two gifted children in the classroom are most often overlooked in planning because so many others have more glaring academic needs. Parents of the gifted can advocate at their children's schools for *cluster grouping*—a grouping method in which schools group five to eight gifted students in a general classroom with a teacher who has professional development in the learning needs and the methods of teaching gifted students. A pull-out program, where the gifted spend an hour or less in enrichment outside the classroom once or twice a week, is helpful but not sufficient. Gifted students have needs beyond one or two hours a week in an enrichment program and cluster grouping allows them to be served in the general classroom as well.

It should be noted that ability grouping—in this instance *cluster grouping*—is not the same as the educational practice known as *tracking*. Tracking can be quite detrimental to student self-esteem and self-efficacy, in that it divides students into distinct groups (i.e., low, middle, and high) for the whole day for *all* instruction. Ability grouping differs from tracking in that it groups students for a part of the school day (i.e., for a lesson or a portion of a lesson) and directs the educational activities to the specific abilities of the clustered group. Hailey would have definitely been clustered in a highly able group in language arts and perhaps science, but not necessarily in other academic areas.

A final approach that parents might consider for their gifted daughters who are at risk of what might be termed "going underground" with their abilities is mentoring. Chapter 3 explored the different types of mentoring and how to set up a mentoring relationship. Mentoring is establishing an ongoing relationship with a professional who is expert or leader in an area of interest to the gifted student. The mentor introduces the student to his or her profession, answers career exploration questions, allows the student to shadow him or her while the mentor is engaged in professional activities, and may even provide occasions for the student to collaborate in research or practice in the field. In light of what we learned from Brown and Gilligan, when mentoring occurs with successful women as the mentors, relationships give gifted girls the opportunity to journey toward their adult selves accompanied by caring adults who can model decision making, resilience, and other strengths.

Hailey's parents noticed the changes in their daughter, who was beginning to shut down in terms of her achievement motivation in order to fit in with classmates and to escape their teasing and threats. Hoping to draw on their daughter's strengths and interests as a way to keep her in touch with her love of learning, they suggested she talk to the town librarian about volunteering in the library on Saturday mornings. The librarian was delighted to have Hailey read stories to the younger children during story hour and invited her to take part in an upcoming storytelling workshop with a professional author. Although Hailey was younger than other participants in the workshop, they shared her love of language and writing and readily accepted her. The author soon noticed her writing strengths as Hailey read some of her compositions from her journal and offered to mentor her with her fiction writing. The two of them spent time in the library each weekend sharing their writing and giving each other feedback. The active mentoring relationship was mutually beneficial, as Hailey learned as much about herself as she did about the writer's craft and her mentor had a bright young student to critique her children's stories.

Hailey's parents also requested a conference with her teacher and other school officials where they shared information about Hailey's development and activities outside of school and their concerns about her present lack of motivation in school. As a result of the conversation, Mrs. C., sent her recommendation of Hailey to the gifted coordinator. Hailey was accepted into the program and plans were made for her to be placed the following year in a classroom with a clustered group of students gifted in creativity and language arts. All parties agreed to continue to meet regularly to discuss her progress and to consider other services as the need arose.

Reflective Research in the Classroom

1. Do a reflective analysis of the teaching and learning in your classroom using the elements of Connected Teaching.

   • Incorporating personal individual experience

   • Nurturing thoughts to maturity through consensus

   • Basing teacher's authority on cooperation

   • Midwife model of education

2. Where are your strengths?

3. What are your needs?

4. How will you use your strengths to address your needs?

5

The Resilient Self

Laykesha's Voice

"*O*f six living generations, I am from only the second generation to read and write. And I can do anything that I put my heart into," Laykesha, an African-American young woman from the coastal South, relates. She continues by describing how her mother encouraged her to learn and to challenge herself as a young child. At school, even when her classmates teased her for being so studious, calling her a "teacher's pet," she persisted. She loved learning and set her goals high, intent on being the first college graduate in her family. Now, as a sixteen-year-old early entrance college student, a thousand miles from family and the familiar, she maintains her determination in spite of the academic challenge and the new environment. I ask her, "Where does your resilience come from?" Laykesha replies, "It's in me, it's my inner strength. It allows me to be me, who I am, even when others want to change me."

Resilience

Resilience is the ability to rebound from difficulty and learn new ways to cope (Dixon, Hickey, & Dixon, 1992). One researcher wrote of the stress process of academically gifted adolescents. The process consists of an event, a mental appraisal that the event is beyond one's ability to cope, and a response to the stress of the event—either physical or psychological (Baker, 1996).

Malena, another African-American young woman in the early entrance program, is a close friend of Laykesha's. It should be noted that the students in the academy are high-school aged. Most are the age of high school seniors, but a few are younger. However, because they have matriculated as first-year college students, they are eligible for financial aid. A significant portion of the students receive aid.

Coming from a large, southern city, Malena reflected on the process of coping and resilience when she explained that life at a small college in a very rural area of the Northeast was a big adjustment from high school and from her way of life until then. However, she felt that responsibilities she had carried as a child of divorce and as a big sister to step-siblings had taught her how to dig down deep to find the resources to meet her goals.

Resilience reveals itself in the lives of successful young women as their ability to persevere in the face of emotional, physical, and social obstacles that could otherwise hamper their development and achievement of personal goals. Obstacles that gifted girls may face are many. Some are:

- Failure of families and schools to recognize their giftedness.
- Failure of schools to acknowledge and accommodate their needs.
- Societal attitudes toward academic giftedness in girls and acceleration.
- Lack of understanding of their high sensitivity and overexcitabilities.
- Unchallenging and often hostile learning environments.

We are not born with resilience; it is a healthy part of one's psychological development that we learn through modeling and practice (Patterson & Kelleher, 2005). Despite difficulties, successful gifted women are able to develop skills that enhance their ability to persist. They face adversity and recover from it with improved resilience. Patterson and Kelleher describe a cycle of resilience that individuals experience as a series of stages in which they adapt, recover, and grow. Following a difficult event, there is a decline in self-belief. Those who have developed positive ways to handle difficulties are able to adapt and make the necessary changes to recover from the setback. As they recover from the initial blow, they develop stress-management strategies that allow them to return to a healthy stress level. Through the practice of active reflection, they grow from new knowledge that comes from the three stages—adapting, recovering, and growing.

Resilience, Coping, and Versatility

An important aspect in developing resilience is the ability to learn and to practice effective coping. Individuals react to stressful situations in different ways. Individuals may choose from several coping strategies (Mattlin, Wethington, & Kessler, 1990). The choices of strategies and the actions that represent them are as follows.

Coping Strategy	Coping Action
• Avoidance	Do something to avoid thinking about the problem.
• Positive reappraisal	Think about the problem in a way that makes it seem less stressful.
• Religion	Use religious beliefs to cope.
• Active cognitive	Think about how to solve the problem.
• Active behavioral	Do something to solve the problem.
• Social support	Talk to someone about the problem.
• Versatile coping	Use of more than one strategy.

Of those listed above, effective strategies for dealing with everyday stressors in the environment are *active behavioral*, *versatile coping*, and *religion*, which is most beneficial with loss of a loved one. In my own work, I find that *social support* is a crucial piece of versatile coping for females.

Current research in cognitive-behavioral therapy suggests that it can be very effective in altering negative thinking which may lead to depression and other disorders (Begley, 2007). The neuroplasticity of the brain means that activities of the brain and its structure can change depending on the individual's cognitive response to experience. Thus, with mindful attention, individuals can create connections in the brain that positively influence their reactions to stressful or negative events. Relaxation and meditation can assist the individual in changing perspectives regarding negative stressors in the environment. In effect, by changing the brain's circuitry, we can practice more effective coping.

The least effective coping strategies are *avoidance* of the problem, *active cognitive* coping, which is thinking about the problem but not acting on it, and *positive reappraisal*, deciding that the problem is not as bad as it seemed. However, when combined as part of versatile coping, active cognitive and reappraisal are effective ways to respond to stress (Mattlin, Wethington, & Kessler, 1990). Thus, a scenario of successful coping through the use of versatile strategies might be similar to the following scenario. A gifted young woman experiences a stressful event. Because of her keen thinking ability, she begins to sort through the event in her mind (active cognitive). At that point she may call a friend to talk about the situation (social support). The act of sharing the problem releases some of the pent up anxiety she is feeling, and she reappraises the situation (positive reappraisal), coming up with some ideas about how she will act on her decisions (active behavioral).

Effective Versatile Coping

- Active cognitive   Thinking about the problem.
- Cognitive appraisal   Changing one's perspective.
- Social support   Talking with friends or family.
- Active behavioral   Acting on the problem.

Young women who are successful in dealing with the effects of stress reveal versatile coping patterns. I have found resilient students in various environments who demonstrate their versatile coping abilities in a number of ways. They have expressed their willingness to separate from family and friends in an effort to pursue needed educational opportunities; they display the courage in the face of sexual threats and harassment; and they reject rigid perceptions of themselves as students, preferring instead to act in multifaceted ways as practicing professionals. Jacqueline, a student in an early college entrance program, summarized the feelings of her peers when she stated, "There are so many men here and they are all here for engineering. And it's not a very diverse environment. I felt during my year here that this was something I had to overcome. I had this feeling that overcoming the environment helped with self-efficacy." The students also spoke of past coping with difficult home or school environments. As Malena told me, "When you were raised to raise other people, where there was pressure from everywhere, where you weren't getting the attention that you needed but always had to take care of things, it's definitely a lot harder." Self-belief among the students was strong, and they demonstrated success with versatile coping.

Z-I-N Breathing—A Stress Break

- Help students to practice this strategy for relieving stress and regaining focus during the day.
- Z-I-N stands for "Zero in Now."
- Z—Take a deep breath, hold it for a few seconds and exhale slowly. As you exhale, consciously relax your head, neck, shoulders and arms.
- I—Take a second deep, cleansing breath, and this time, relax head, neck, shoulders and trunk as you exhale.
- N—Take a final deep breath and relax head to toe. Concentrate on letting go of any remaining stress and affirm your ability to accomplish the task before you.
- Continue your activity, refreshed and calm.

Students I have known present themselves as not merely academic students. Rather, they speak of their involvement in athletics and extracurricular activities. These, as well as their work experiences—such as on the family farm, at a veterinarian's office, or in a daycare center—provided them with life skills that enriched their repertoire of abilities. The chance for girls to build a social support system with other girls like themselves is crucial to the strengthening of their resilience.

Many students I work with have the opportunity to work as a practicing professional as high school students. Often this work involves authentic experiences in the field, working with mentors who are experts in the student's field of interest. For example, Malena worked during the summer as a volunteer in a hospital. She was part of the team of social workers and was supervised and assisted by experts. She glowed when she told me, "I even had my own beeper!" Eve, a student in a private school, spent time each week at the local public television station as a member of the camera crew. Her sister student, Heidi, worked as a hospice volunteer. Other students participate in summer enrichment camps on university campuses, performing research or enhancing their creativity through work in the fine and performing arts. All of these experiences, along with their experiences in enriched environments, give them a sense of versatility as practicing professionals.

An excellent strategy for self-understanding is the activity *Collaborative Coping Skills Group* (see page 45). In addition to self-introspection, participants are able to collaborate and to learn effective coping from each other. Bringing together a group of gifted girls to share and practice coping strategies allows them to form relationships and at the same time develop their unique voice and coping skills.

Collaborative Coping Skills Group

An activity for school counselors:
- After gathering a group of four to six highly able middle school or high school students together, seat them in a circle in a comfortable and quiet environment.
- Explain that the goal of the activity is for students to learn about how they handle stressful situations and to share and learn from one another.
- Tell the students that they are going to be asked to review a scenario. They will first visualize it and converse afterward.
- Ask them to be authentic with themselves, answering the questions as they *truly* think, not as they think they *should* think.
  - Think about a normal day you experienced recently. How did you feel? What was it like?
  - Now think about a stressful event that happened to you on a day like this. What happened? How did you react? How did you feel physically?
  - Did you feel angry, frustrated, anxious? If none of these, what emotions did you feel? How did that make you feel about yourself?
  - How did you cope with this event? What did you do to relieve the stress? What effect did your actions have on you? On the situation?
  - How do you feel now? What will you do in the future if you encounter a similar situation?
  - What did you learn from this exercise? In what ways are you growing stronger?
- After the students have visualized and silently reflected on the questions, read each of them again and allow time between each one for them to discuss. Explain that if they are uncomfortable, they do not have to share, and they may feel better about speaking as the conversation progresses. Invite anyone who wants to come back later and talk with you individually to do so.

- As students mention effective coping skills (active cognitive, cognitive appraisal, social support, active behavioral), give positive affirmation with statements like, "Talking with friends or family is a good way to cope." Allow them to *construct* the effective skills by building on effective coping reactions that they used.
- Before reading the last question that asks what they learned, bring out a wide, gold colored ribbon that is more than long enough to encircle the group.
- Explain to them that the color gold symbolizes strength in Eastern cultures and that they have grown stronger and have helped each other to grow stronger as a result of their collaboration.
- Hold one end of the ribbon and pass it to the right behind the back of the girl beside you to her right hand. Then ask her the final question: *In what ways are you growing stronger?*
- After she answers, she passes the ribbon behind and to the right hand of the next girl, who gives her answer. As earlier in the exercise, a student can choose not to respond.
- Each girl passes the end of the ribbon behind the next girl so that in the end they are all encircled in a ribbon of strength. Explain to them that when they encounter stressful situations in the future they can recall this group and know that they have the support of caring girls like themselves.
- Serve light refreshments after the discussion to allow for the students to continue to socialize and build relationships.

Personal Factors and Resilience

Resilience? It's in me, it's my inner strength. It allows me to be me, even when others want to change me.

—LAYKESHA

Studies identify a clear sense of Self, strong self-belief, and persistence in pursuing one's goals as common characteristics among gifted females who demonstrate strong resilience (Noble, Subotnik & Arnold, 1999; Reis, 2002). I recall the profoundly gifted Katie, who told me when she was five years old that she was committed to a career in medicine. Her parents agreed, and told me that at two years old she reported that she planned to be a pediatric neurosurgeon. She demonstrated early on that she was aware of who she was and believed in her ability to accomplish her goals. As she accelerated through the school system, she persisted in her self-belief despite several obstacles along the way. Later, as an eleven-year-old college student, she served on a research team at a well-recognized medical research center. The resilience she developed along the way assists her in her studies and in sustaining the energy she needs to persist.

What personal factors do resilient females possess that enhance their success when confronted with difficulties and stress? How can educators and other caring adults assist girls in the development of personal factors of success? Patterson and Keller (2005), in addressing resilience in school leaders, identify three sources that aid in its development: personal values, personal efficacy, and personal energy. A similar framework is useful as we examine successful facets of resilience in gifted females.

Facets of Resilience

- Ethic of caring
- Self-acceptance
- Entelechy
- Efficacy
- Vitality

Ethic of Caring

Central to the personal values of highly able females I know is the full acceptance of their gifts. As Chapter 4 explored, our gifted girls are in jeopardy of losing their belief in themselves and their voice due to the pressure to conform. They may try to become inconspicuous in terms of their abilities in schools where minimum proficiency may be the rule.

I think of Cameron, who grew up and attended public schools in a small, yet diverse southern city. A gifted musician, mathematician, and leader, her strong spiritual center affects all that she does—church and community service, youth leadership and more. As a middle school student, Cameron was the subject of teasing and taunts from students and teachers, who said she would fit in better if she had less intellectual drive. Despite the social pressure, Cameron persisted, finding avenues beyond the classroom—summer enrichment programs and community leadership—to feed her gifts. When given a choice, she elected to switch school districts to a public high school where her academics, leadership, and personal drive were encouraged. In that environment, her belief in Self was affirmed and celebrated, and she achieved recognition throughout the state and nationally. She currently attends a rigorous Ivy League university.

Self-Acceptance

A second aspect of our gifted girls' personal values is acceptance of their femaleness. In other words, rather than considering it a limitation to be female, they delight in it. They take utmost advantage of the ethic of caring that Gilligan (1982) identified as a higher sense of moral responsibility. Our girls respond to a directive to care, to address the needs of others and of their world. Anna, in an early college entrance academy, explained, "As far as female emotions go, I don't see that they should be looked upon as a weakness at all. Emotions are what make us—instead of being only the scientist or only the technician—they're what make us human beings. And they're what make us relate to each another. And they, a lot of times, make us feel the greatest sense of self-efficacy when we relate to other people and when we help other people."

Entelechy

Entelechy—a word of Greek origin which connotes a drive in an individual to realize one's goals and achieve one's inner agenda—is a third characteristic which my work with gifted females reveals to be vital in developing resilience. Examples of women who responded to an intrinsic calling are Sandra Day O'Connor (Supreme Court justice), Maya Angelou (author), Eleanor Roosevelt (human rights activist), Ellen Ochoa (astronaut), and Mother Teresa (servant of the poor). Paz, from Spain, calls it her "life force" and spoke of how it was her imperative to fulfill her authentic Self. In another instance, Brigid—an early middle school student—came to me and proposed a collaborative project with another girl that would help gifted students in elementary school understand who they were as individuals and what potential they had to change their world. Her presentation was eventually presented to an international audience of gifted educators.

Today she is involved in planning green housing and plays a key role in the environmental and aesthetic development in a large metropolitan city. Throughout the years that I mentored and observed her growth, an intensity of purpose reflected Brigid's passion to make the world a better place.

Efficacy

Although explored in more depth in Chapter 7, a gifted girl's efficacy—the belief in her ability to impact her world and effect change—is a key facet in the development of resilience. The self-understanding that she can set a goal, organize herself, and gather the necessary resources to accomplish the task, strengthens her determination and her perseverance when she encounters obstacles. Katie, at six years old, started her own make-a-difference fund, with the proceeds dedicated to helping families with no medical insurance in receiving health care. Malena shared a client load as a volunteer social worker at a local hospital. Cameron attended a student state assembly one year and came back determined to be elected to the top office the next year—and she was! A major factor in all of these successes was self-efficacy. Their "I can!" attitude permitted them to set goals and pursue their passions.

Vitality

Vitality presents itself in varied ways in gifted females. For Paz, it is what she calls her *chispa de vida*—spark of life. For Brigid, it is her intensity. For Anna, it is her gentle, ethically grounded self-affirmation. For Lilly, it is the boundless delight she expresses while performing ballet. The characteristics of vitality, drive, and inner spirit ground the girls in their gifts and are ever present in their behavior. Through vitality they demonstrate strength of Self, of knowing who they are, what they are capable of, and their determination to be fully authentic. In some girls—Lilly, for example—it reveals itself in their creativity. In others—Hailey—it springs from her rich reservoir of words to become intensity of language. In Caroline, it is her eager fascination with the natural world. Laykesha's perky "can do" attitude exudes vitality.

The vital force that flings our gifted girls into life and sustains them through adversity needs to be recognized and nourished, if they are to become resilient adolescents and young adults. Considering the pure energy that many display, they are at risk of being labeled as having behavior problems or misdiagnosed with an attention disorder. With caring adults who affirm and praise their intensities, girls will learn to reveal their spirit and tap into it as they confront various dilemmas in their lives.

Nurturing Resilience

It is essential that girls on the path of developing resilience recognize and listen to their inner voice. Through knowing one's voice girls and young women develop their self-knowledge, self-belief, and self-efficacy. The previous chapter addressed how keeping a journal promotes the development of voice in gifted girls. We have also explored the importance of mentors, who model strong problem solving, coping, and resiliency skills. These are important sources of resilience knowledge. What are other ways to assist girls to become capable in the face of adversity?

Access to books about other highly able girls and women through biography is a superb resource. Historical, contemporary, and fictional biographies are all appealing. Successful women whom girls encounter in books are often their first role models. Though decades have passed, I still remember reading my first biography about a historical woman of accomplishment—Clara Barton, founder of the Red Cross. For the first time, I experienced the realization that women had the ability to fulfill themselves and achieve great deeds. From biographies, girls learn about goal-setting and career paths. They see how other females confront challenges and develop resilience. Books that address women of diverse ethnic and social backgrounds are essential for all students and are especially effective for gifted girls from diverse cultures. The Chapter 10 resources give suggestions for books that parents and teachers might consider.

Movies about capable girls and young women who confront difficulties and use their strong reasoning and resilience to find solutions are a very effective way to model resiliency skills to our highly able girls. In the *Chronicles of Narnia* movies, Lucy is a strong example of how resilience is developed over time. The *Harry Potter* series features the brilliant Hermione, a young woman with well-defined goals who endures teasing and bullying, yet manages to persevere toward her purpose. For older girls, an example of a great movie about developing resilience is *Akeelah and the Bee* (2006), in which eleven-year-old

Akeelah—an African-American inner city girl—tries not to reveal her abilities so she can fit in with other students. When she wins the school spelling bee and starts to prepare for the regional competition, she begins to listen to her inner voice and finds that she needs to draw on her strengths and develop life skills. A poignant and magical story of Fiona, a young Irish girl who tries to unravel family tragedies and in the quest finds her authentic Self, is *The Secret of Roan Inish* (1994). This is a wonderful family film that will open children to another culture and the importance of family stories. Another story of self-discovery is the movie *An American Rhapsody* (2001). Suzanne was raised by foster parents in her native Hungary for her first six years, after her parents were forced to flee the communist regime. Reunited with her family in California, she grows up questioning who she really is and where she belongs. As a teenager, she travels back to Budapest and there makes peace with her own, authentic Self.

In this chapter several needs and services for our female students emerge. Laykesha, Malena, and all of our girls need to tap into what Laykesha describes as her inner strength. Drawing on their principled and vigorous core, they can learn effective coping and resiliency skills from parents and educators who model them. Adults can provide resources through books and other media that will help girls to see others like themselves who face and solve life problems. Additionally, counselors can create collaborative communities in which girls can explore their inner voice and support each other in developing a common ethic of caring. Our gifted girls are constantly bombarded with messages that address the importance of body image, the pressure to hide their abilities, and suppression of their authentic voices in order to fit into the mainstream. It is vital that they hear the message that healthy and joyful adults are those who learn to be true to who they are.

Reflective Research in the Classroom

1. Think of a recent stressful event that you experienced in your life.

2. How did you react to the event?

3. Which coping strategies did you use?

4. Were they effective strategies, based on your learning in the chapter?

5. Are there more effective strategies you could have used? If so, how might that have affected your resilience?

6. Based on this reflection, in what ways can you model effective coping strategies in the classroom? What effects might this modeling have on particular students' needs?

6

Autonomy and Affiliation

Melori's Voice

Melori is a student in a private high school designed to develop aware-ness of how students learn best and to develop thinking in ways that serve them best as lifelong learners. A significant percentage of the students attend the school on scholarships. Melori and three of her sister students con-verse with me at the school. I notice that even though she is recently arrived from Malaysia, she expresses herself fluently and interacts warmly with her peers. She is a gentle, yet intense, young woman who shares her thoughts and feelings freely.

One of the girls begins to talk about how they enjoy studying and inter-relating with other students at the school who share their love for learning and other interests. Equally important to them is the one afternoon each week when they are allowed to work on individual inquiry and community-based learning. For example, one of the girls works with hospice and another is learning television production skills at the local public television studio. Melori tells me that the opportunity to develop her own inquiry project, find the necessary resources to support it through collaboration with others, implement it, and carry it through to completion gives her a sense of auton-omy that allows her to feel she will be capable as a professional.

Her friend Vanessa shifts the conversation to a more personal topic. She is a commuter at the school and must drive quite a distance in the morning and afternoon. Although she thrives on the relationships that collaboration with her teachers and peers allows, she tells me of how important her time on the road is to her as it allows her to be alone with herself and reflect on who she is and how the new experiences of each day affect her. Melori chimes in that she has the same vital need to be alone, to find her inner peace and to center herself. I ask, "Where do you find that space?" She replies, "In my room. My room is sacred."

Autonomy

As a gifted young woman, Melori has a psychological need to simultaneously develop her sense of autonomy and forge collaborative connections with others. Miller (1986) described this important construct—autonomy—as the need to become self-directed. Furthermore, she describes how the male model of autonomy, which society admires as the quality of the "rugged individual," does not suit the woman who is fully aware of being autonomous and who recognizes at the same time that it is her very autonomy that gives her a fuller potential to form relationships with others.

It's up to me, and if I don't do something, then that's a lost opportunity.
—MALENA

Young gifted women speak of their need to feel autonomous, often at the same time that they emphasize their need for close relationships with others. Their successes, indeed their abilities to function effectively in their environments, depend on their skill and their freedom to continually perform a dance of approach and distance. Miller (1986) wrote that women experience a constant process in developing their own creative autonomy. The practice involves always being open to perceive her changing Self and to understand Self as a participant in the world. Melori and her friends reveal their awareness of their developing vision of Self and for their need to personally create an autonomous Self in relationship to the world. This construct reflects three important developmental facets: the strength of individual voice, one's awareness of the need to connect with others, and a strong sense of one's individual autonomy.

Autonomous Learner

Experiences with highly able girls reveal many who realize the importance of being an autonomous learner. In public school, Brenda expressed the concept as, "I feel most capable when I can understand and I can do it on my own; and I don't need anybody else to help me . . . when I feel sensible and I feel strong enough that I can do it on my own." Other students in her environment expressed the need to feel that their own efforts and abilities alone were a significant factor in their learning. For example, when Bridget solved a difficult math problem over several minutes and looked back on her work with satisfaction; when Darcie realized that she had demonstrated the expertise needed to affect the learning of one of her young charges at the daycare center; when Gail's responsibility and ability were recognized by her parents and she was left in charge of the family farm; in each of these situations, the girls all felt a sense of autonomous efficacy.

Autonomy in early college entrance programs manifests itself as a strong belief in Self and a strong sense of efficacy. Students are acutely aware of the autonomy and the self-agency they enjoyed in managing their own resources, in regulating their energy and time, and in their efforts to achieve a balance between academics and connectedness. As autonomous learners, they separated themselves from their home and high school environments and set their own high standards of achievement in a new and challenging environment. In Anna's words, "I think a lot of it is that going to school in an environment where you're on your own, where you're living as well as going to school . . . it brings a focus on learning not only about classroom and about topics and stuff, but it's kind of just living in general."

Similarly, Malena, an African-American from a southern state who was almost a thousand miles from home, affirmed, "It's up to me, and if I don't do something, then that's a lost opportunity." Jacqueline, who was developing her voice as a visual artist, spoke of coming to the realization that creating art is an intimate and private process that can't be totally shared with others, despite its public purpose. She desired her art to be a medium of communication that expresses her own unique Self. Malena spoke for many of her peers when she told of arriving at the university as a young student. "I was intimidated at first. Then, I just took time out for Malena, and worked on Malena and what Malena wanted. I notice now that I have a solid foundation of who I am and what I want to do."

Qualities of an Autonomous Learner

- Self-awareness of Self as learner.
- Self-directed learner.
- Manages resources.
- Understands effort-success relationship.
- Prefers independent problem solving.

In Melori's private school environment, the impulse toward becoming an autonomous learner manifested itself as each individual student achieved a degree of *metacognition*—thinking about thinking and learning about learning. Each student reported how she learned best, and this knowledge gave each of them confidence as a learner. Statements that reflected this self-awareness were like Vanessa's, when she explained to me, "I learn the best when it's my own language or when I can translate into my [learning] language. That's why I learn the best in a one-on-one situation, or a small class."

Self-Regulated Learning

Self-regulated learning is the learner's ability to set goals, organize, and learn in ways that best suit the student's strengths. It involves a series of skills, which can be taught within or outside of the classroom. Because the learner herself tailors skills and learning in a manner that reflects the individual learning profile, self-regulation significantly improves the chances for success at any different learning task. Vanessa understands that she needs to interpret material to be learned in such a way that she can personalize it. Also, she knows that the learning environment that suits her best is a seminar style class. Laykesha, who we met in Chapter 5, organized herself at the desk in the large lecture hall of her college biology class with her notebook in front of her, text notes she had made from the reading assignment, a glossary of terms, text and other resources. As the lecture and discussion continued, she highlighted certain parts of her text notes, added to her glossary of terms, copied visual aids and other drawings from the board, and took notes. She told me after the class that she keeps a strict agenda of her assignments and schedules the time needed for completing work in all her courses *before* she puts anything else on her schedule. Each of these learners self-regulates according to her unique learning needs.

Self-regulation is a vital component of developing as an autonomous learner and many gifted students are ready to learn self-regulated learning strategies much earlier than others. If we consider the fact that a significant number of gifted students enter school reading and doing math operations, we may have preschoolers who have already developed the individual strategies necessary for early mastery of print and numbers. Nevertheless, not all students will naturally self-regulate, so it is important that educators and parents teach and model these important skills.

Self-Regulated Learning Skills

A self-regulated learner is one who:
- Sets learning goals.
- Organizes learning tasks.
- Manages time conscientiously.
- Collects and records information competently.
- Practices critical reading skills.
- Efficiently prepares for exams.
- Effectively plans, drafts and revises papers.
- Evaluates work accurately.
- Reflects on and improves the skills above.

Strong, self-regulated learners know efficient ways to organize, evaluate, and order their study skills and resources. Laykesha demonstrated personal strategies as she set her personal goals, organized her time and materials, used note-taking and other resources wisely, and reflected and evaluated the success of her strategies. Self-regulated learning is the strongest academic characteristic of successful girls that I observed in my almost four decades in education.

Educators can assist students in developing the ability to self-regulate. The suggested strategy that follows, *Self-Regulated Learning Exercise*, enables students to set goals, organize the resources to accomplish those goals, and set clear procedures for completing them successfully. Additionally, the *Efficacy Estimate* and the *Actual Efficacy* scores allow the students to self-evaluate their belief in their ability to accomplish a goal. The successful completion of a task has a positive effect on an individual's self-efficacy. As a result, students set higher goals for themselves *and* have a better success rate in accomplishing their goals (Bandura, 1997).

Self-Regulated Learning Exercise

- *Goal-setting*: During opening time in the classroom allow time for students to reflect on what they need to accomplish during the day.
- *Recording*: Then state what your own personal goal for the day is. Students then write their goal in their Learning Log (see Appendix B). Invite students to share their goals if they wish.
- *Organizing*: Based on the goal of each student, ask each one to think about the time and materials needed to meet the individual goal. Students then write those needs in their Learning Log. Explain to them that they do not necessarily need to use all the spaces and can add more information as needed.
- *Procedures*: Ask students to list what steps they need to take in order to complete their daily goal. Again, explain to them that they do not necessarily need to use all the spaces and can add more steps if needed.
- *Efficacy Estimate*: At this point, ask students to fill in their Efficacy Estimate. Explain to them that this means that as a result of looking at their goal statement, their organization and their procedures list, how successful they think they will be in completing the project. The teacher can ask them to note this estimate as a percentage score, on a numeric scale (e.g., 1–5), or as a term (e.g., Excellent, Very Good).
- *Task completion*: Students can check off steps as they complete them.
- *Actual Efficacy*: At the end of the day have students review their Learning Log sheet and rate themselves in terms of their Actual Efficacy, which rates their success in meeting their goal.
- *Self-Evaluation*: It is a good practice for students to self-evaluate the quality of their work using a rubric, which the teacher provides prior to an assignment.

Self-belief, goal-setting, success in organizing and accomplishing challenging learning on their own—all of these perceptions and abilities contribute to nurturing autonomy in gifted females. Because we understand that they are at risk of hiding their abilities in order to fit in, or doubting that they are truly gifted, caring adults and educators can assist them early by teaching self-regulation skills. Although some of our highly able males and females appear to acquire these skills on their own, they are skills that can be taught and applied in the classroom at an early age. All students will benefit from self-regulated learning strategies and strengthened self-efficacy; for our gifted daughters, they are crucial.

Collaboration

Collaboration signifies a participatory style in which leaders and team members are enriched through listening and discussion (Navan, 1994). It is a key attribute in the successful development of gifted females. To collaborate means to co-labor, and educators are now recognizing what business leaders have known for some time: We are social beings and our best work comes from the active participation of all (Harasim, 1991). Gifted girls, and other students as well, thrive in a participatory, collaborative environment of teaching and learning. Teaching and enriching others, positive reinforcement by teachers and peers, and forming close relationships in a small school or classroom environment are all important characteristics of learning settings where collaboration develops and flourishes.

Characteristics of Collaborative Classrooms

- Teachers model collaboration by inviting colleagues into the classroom for collaborative instruction.
- Teachers are collaborative role models, asking for ideas from students and involving them in group decision making.
- Teachers use collaborative grouping and learning strategies that allow students to construct learning together.
- Students have the opportunity to be partners in designing and caring for the learning environment.
- Students collaborate with teachers in creating classroom rules and consequences.
- Students apply self-regulated learning strategies and assist their peers in developing self-regulation by sharing their successes.
- Students are engaged as members of a learning community and perceive themselves as vital participants.

Affiliation

Successful women celebrate Self and their unique abilities when they use feelings to relate to others. As one gifted young woman told me, "It is what makes us not just the scientist, or not just the engineer. It is what makes us human. I think that it is important in feeling that you communicate with people, touch other people, and basically relate to them." Her words echo the findings of Brown and Gilligan (1992) regarding the need for connected relationships. Malena, from an early college entrance program, told me that she and Jacqueline were roommates. They were from different regions of the country, different family backgrounds, and different ethnicities. They commented that they had very little in common and did not communicate much before their participation in our conversations. After their collaboration with me on a project, Malena said that they and other students spoke of how they were changed by the opportunity to participate in the research. Malena said that the group gathered periodically and continued to explore the questions and ideas that they pondered during the interviews and visits, which became the springboard for more growth and connectedness. As Brown and Gilligan (1992) experienced in their research, I am changed also through my work with gifted girls and young women and continue to gain new perspectives regarding their needs and my own life choices.

In a private school environment the gifted young women emphasized how collaboration assisted the growth of their own metacognitive processes. Eve spoke of being grounded in her interactions with others and how her learning and behavior grew from the interactions. Her peers agreed enthusiastically. Heidi said, "I think that when something gets my attention, or I get interested in it, it will stay with me longer when I can relate it to some other experience, and talk about it. That helps me remember things." Vanessa adds later, "I kind of use my own personal memories, like I always, I live in the past too much . . . But I kind of use what I'm learning and I apply it to what happened to me and kind of use the memory as knowledge for the future." When I observed Vanessa in class, I noticed how she uses memories and experiences to converse and develop consensus with her classmates.

Gallos (1995) emphasized the need for supportive and encouraging learning settings in a study regarding the characteristics of ethical and caring environments. In all educational environments students demonstrate their need for close, relational learning.

Students feel supported in this need by warm and supportive faculty and staff. They speak of certain teachers who took a special interest in them. Without dedicated educators to support and nurture the students in the college setting, the university environments would most likely be overwhelming and difficult for highly sensitive, gifted students.

Students speak of the warm and supportive family environments that some schools create as an important part of their perception of capability. Laykesha explained, "Here, I have a lot of people to fall back on, like I have Malena; I have so many people here who are just willing to be there for me." Malena agreed and added, "At home, I didn't have a lot of emotional support or encouragement, and I was getting a lot of negative vibes. And it's like, I got here, and it's really nice to have the emotional support and I try to give that much back."

The need to study with like peers—students who are of similar abilities and motivation—is essential for gifted students. In public school, girls tell of the difficulty that they encounter in heterogeneously grouped classes with teachers who do not carry through with challenging objectives when less capable or less motivated students ignore or fail to meet learning and homework expectations. Gifted young women in that environment feel less capable in such classes, regardless of their high grades, believing that in the college environment they will be found lacking in subjects where they do not have sufficient challenge in high school. On the other hand, gifted girls feel most efficacious when a teacher sets challenging expectations and works with the class to ensure that all students apply themselves. In the case of upper-level math and science classes, there tends to be a certain degree of homogeneous grouping of like peers. Due to the level of difficulty of the classes of this kind, the more capable students choose to study them and the less prepared or less motivated students avoid them. It is important that parents and teachers urge their daughters to take the higher level courses without worrying about grades. The more rigorous requirements in Advanced Placement and honors courses not only prepare the students for college study, but many college admissions offices are more impressed by students who are willing to take academic risks.

Those students who choose challenging early entrance and honors university programs report similar perceptions. Their choice of the college environment is in large part made in order to study with more capable and more task-committed, motivated students. Being in an environment with more able students reinforces their own sense of efficacy. Students relate how studying with like peers—especially sharing the learning ethic of teachers and other students—enhances their belief in their abilities. They prosper in a setting in which all—teachers, students and staff—are invested in developing metacognition, self-regulation, and personal growth.

Supportive Learning Environments

- Provide an open and welcoming setting.
- Encourage students to collaborate and connect with others.
- Have faculty and staff that understand unique needs of the gifted and respond to those needs.
- Affirm a clear learning ethic.
- Define a level of challenge within a framework of support.
- Emphasize personal growth.

The voices of gifted females underscore how gifted young women perceive themselves as capable academically through autonomous learning experiences. They grow as practicing professionals through inquiry experiences. These modes of learning promote the development of their perceptions of Self as agent, and agency has the potential of becoming the core construct in their future development and success. Chapter 9 explores the concept of agency in depth.

An effective program when working with gifted elementary and middle students is CABLE, an acronym for Career and Business Leadership Experience. CABLE responds to the highly able student's need for early role models and career exploration. The ongoing mentoring experience enables young students to connect with a leader in a career field of interest to them. Over a period of one or more years, the students meet informally at school with their designated role model to talk about their interests and learn about how the female leader assigned to them organizes her daily work life, makes decisions, and resolves problems. At least twice a year, the student visits the workplace of her mentor and shadows her through the day.

Career and Business Leadership Experience (CABLE)

- Make a list of successful leaders and other professional women in your community.
- Make a list of girls in your gifted program who will benefit from the CABLE experience.
- Compose and send a letter to the women, giving them an overview of the program and inviting their participation.
- Once you receive responses, match them to your female students according to the girls' academic and creative strengths and interests.
- Arrange an evening reception for the professional women, the girls, and their mothers or a significant female relative or adult.
- Plan a very special reception. Make it as fancy as you can so that the girls feel special. Your school, the public library, or a community room are possible locations. Don't forget the name tags!
- When everyone has arrived, share with the group what the goals and activities of the CABLE program are, how the partnerships were chosen, and what the girls will do.
- Introduce the professional women and share their accomplishments.
- Pass out sealed envelopes with a personal note written on fine stationery from the professional mentor to her assigned student.
- The mentor then meets her assigned girl and parent. Allow some time for them to chat.
- End the session with refreshments for all.
- The coordinator of the program then plans and supervises subsequent after school meetings and shadowing experiences.

Successful young gifted women learn and grow through voice, connection, and relational knowing. They develop these qualities in inclusive environments where their teachers and professors model the qualities of authentic inquiry. Behaviorally, our students are self-constructors of knowledge, socially responsible, and grounded in an ethic of caring. They have a keen awareness of their abilities and refuse to attribute their success to luck, as is the case of many gifted females as reported in previous research. Successful young women show strong metacognitive awareness and social-emotional strength. Rather than avoiding math and sciences, girls can feel confident in their abilities in these disciplines. They are risk-takers. Above all, they learn best in collaborative, supportive, learning environments that respond to their need for relational, connected, and self-construction of knowledge. Our gifted daughters participate in a perpetual dance of approach and retreat as they find themselves and their strengths through affiliation, and then withdraw to their sacred space to reflect, thus finding their authenticity. They have learned to negotiate the two spaces—public and private—successfully, and to grow stronger as a result.

Reflective Research in the Classroom

1. Look at the *Characteristics of Collaborative Classrooms* on page 59.

2. Reflect on your classroom in terms of the characteristics

3. Which elements are already present in your classroom?

4. How do they affect the growth and development of all the students?

5. Are there characteristics that you could incorporate into your learning environment?

6. What effect might these changes have on your students' learning and their perceptions about themselves?

7. As a result of this reflection, what actions will you take in terms of your professional practice?

7

Achieving Efficacy

Vanessa's Voice

*V*anessa *wears a polyester flowered shirt and rust colored polyester pants—definitely an outfit out of the early seventies that she may have found in an attic or a secondhand shop. She is in seminar listening to a presentation on homosexuality prepared by one of the Indonesian students in the class. As the student finishes the report and begins to ask for the opinions of others in the class, Vanessa draws on her sketchbook. During the ensuing discussion, she looks up from her drawing from time to time to listen to other students and to contribute thoughts and opinions. Her remarks reflect that she is actively listening and engaged in the discussion. I notice that the other students pay careful attention to all of her observations. She takes the facts and the opinions of others and begins to weave connections to social phenomena and related issues. She ties one peer's thoughts to another's with ease, drawing on her astute critical thinking and precise verbal expression.*

Vanessa expresses strong perceptions of efficacy in various academic subjects and thinking skills. "I can do everything!" This self-belief comes from no specific place. "It's in my Self, my successes, the environment, within me, a lot of things." She feels most efficacious in the awareness of her own individual learning process. "I have my own personal truths and my own explanations. I believe in their [other people's] definitions; I just explain them to myself differently." She knows what works best for her and knows that she has to make her own appropriate choices.

Contextual Knowing

Previous chapters examined key developmental constructs of success: voice, resilience, autonomy, and collaboration. Young women who show strengths in these areas have greater expertise in navigating their world. A woman discovers herself through context and relationships. It is significant that all constructs explored in this book constitute contextualized knowing (Gilligan, 1982). Voice is heard and refined in context. With other constructs—resilience, autonomy, and collaboration—we mediate and strengthen them as a result of factors in the environment that either encourage or threaten them.

Fisher (1999) characterizes this as *web thinking* and describes how women have the knack of weaving the many varied phenomena in their environment into complete, interrelated understandings. Because of their ability to make such connections, women see themselves as individuals-in-relationship. Therefore, development of voice is really voice-in-relationship and becoming a resilient person is actually resilience-in-relationship, and so on. This insight becomes even more helpful when we consider agency and efficacy, which appear in successful women quite differently than they appear in most of their male counterparts. For the majority of males, efficacy and agency are central to the concept of *instrumentality*—the view of Self as an instrument who acts *on* the world, constructs and effects change. By contrast, the model ascribed more to women is that of acting *in* the world in accord with others who, as a group, bring about change in context (Miller, 1986).

Thus far, we have investigated the following critical issues:

- The notable characteristics of able young girls that parents and educators need to understand.
- How this understanding can enable us to assist in their successful development.
- The ways in which able female students develop voice, resilience, autonomy and collaborative skills.
- Strategies that empower personal decision making and career exploration.
- How to create caring environments that respond to the needs of our students.

As we examine the characteristics of efficacy and agency and how they develop in successful young women, I would like to pose an essential question that will be the major focus in the remaining chapters: In what ways can we be collaborators with our gifted girls in their development of other psychological strengths crucial to their development and self-actualization?

Self-Efficacy

I can do everything! It's in my Self, my successes, the environment, within me.

—VANESSA

In the case study narrative of Vanessa, we see that she exhibits what psychologists would describe as strong self-efficacy. She articulates a sound perception of herself as capable of setting challenging goals and accomplishing those goals. Additionally, she realizes that self efficacy is a distinctly individual construct and that it is dependent on the interactions of her thinking, her environment, and her behavior. For gifted girls, the construct of self-efficacy is critical to their achievement and their psychosocial well-being.

I remember Emily and Crystal, who were inseparable friends from fifth grade on. They were bright, enthusiastic, and expressive members of the enrichment program at their school. In middle school both girls demonstrated high ability and creativity. However, Emily was always well organized and motivated, while Crystal showed early signs of procrastination and difficulty in bringing closure to projects. While Emily was the *steady wins the race* plodder, Crystal most often raced at the last minute to study for a test or complete a paper. Both girls continued to show outstanding potential, although Crystal often doubted that reality, suggesting that maybe she was just fooling people.

Beginning high school was an abrupt and exhilarating change for both girls, and they loved the challenges of a new environment with new ideas and subjects. As the second year of high school began, I sensed in both a leveling off of motivation and challenges and suggested that they apply to a foreign exchange program for the opportunity to spend a year abroad during their junior year. They were both chosen as finalists by a local service club and were sponsored by the district council for an exchange experience in Australia. The two young women spent their junior year of high school on opposite sides of the Australian continent. During their last year of high school, they busied themselves with completing graduation requirements and searching for colleges. In the end the two decided to attend the same small college in the Midwest.

Both women prospered in the university environment. Crystal flourished in the expanded social opportunities and friendships. Emily thrived in the academic environment—welcoming the chance to continue, unimpeded, toward her goals. Emily graduated Phi Beta Kappa and went on to graduate school. Crystal dropped out, worked for a number of years, returned to college and completed her Associate degree, and is working on a college degree as a non-traditional student.

Reflecting on these students, I ponder the paths they created. They are two students with similar abilities and educational experiences, yet very differing beliefs in their own abilities. The role of self-belief in Emily's journey was essential to her goal setting, her focus and her achievement. A weaker perception of efficacy on the part of Crystal was a key factor in her development.

Perceptions of Efficacy

Central to Vanessa's and Emily's success is the construct of self-efficacy. The self-perception of ability is an important factor in the learning process and increases the likelihood for successful realization of one's goals. Bandura (1986) defined perceived self-efficacy as the estimation of our abilities to accomplish a task or goal. Efficacy does not measure the skills that an individual has. Rather, it is the degree of success an individual estimates she can achieve in the performance of a task. The belief in the capacity to perform certain activities positively impacts the learner's intellectual, behavioral, and emotional functioning.

Benefits of Individual Efficacy

- **Intellectual Efficacy:** The individual perceives herself as a learner who can master and apply information effectively.
- **Emotional Efficacy:** The individual believes herself capable of understanding and moderating her emotional responses to ensure her well-being.
- **Behavioral Efficacy:** The individual feels capable of acting in a manner consistent with who she is and her unique needs in a variety of contexts.

Characteristics of efficacy behavior include strong coping skills, appropriate reactions to stress, constructive reactions to failure, motivation to achieve, and informed choices regarding careers and other life aspirations (Bandura, 1982).

Female Efficacy Behaviors

- **Coping:** An individual who believes herself to be more capable can form stronger coping skills.
- **Stress:** Stress management increases with feelings of capability and through more effective coping.
- **Reaction to failure:** Instead of blaming her ability, the individual who feels capable is more likely to reflect on what caused the mistake and learn from it.
- **Motivation:** Each success is a motivating factor for future endeavors.
- **Career choices:** With continuing development of efficacy, awareness of one's abilities becomes more task-specific, which enhances career knowledge and choices.
- **Life aspirations:** Efficacy information enhances thinking, career expectations, and general well-being. This allows the individual to set goals that enhance one's personal growth.

An Efficacy Cycle

As previous chapters affirm, these are valued behaviors for successful young women. When girls develop efficacy beliefs their reflective thinking improves, they are more motivated and they set higher goals. Consequently, they are more able to organize and remain committed to tasks that help them realize their goals. Each accomplishment reinforces the perception of competence. Perceived competence in turn increases the gifted girl's incentive and guides her future actions and goal setting. The entire progression reflects the cyclical nature of self-efficacy development. The stronger her efficacy, the more interested she is in continuing to achieve mastery. Figure 7.1 illustrates the process as it affects learning and goal setting of the gifted female (Bandura 1982, 1986, 1995).

Figure 7.1 The Process of Efficacy Development in the Gifted Female

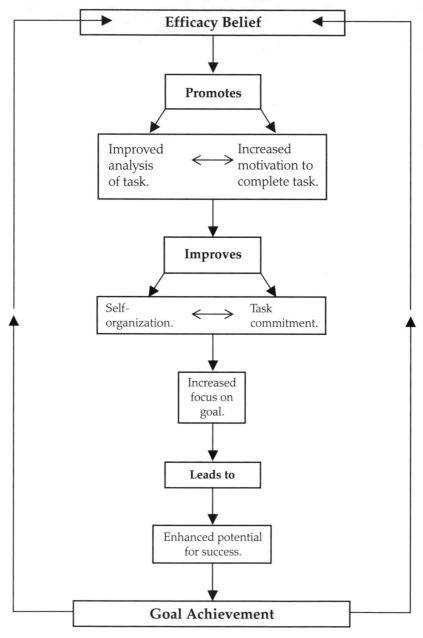

(Navan, 2009)

In the thinking domain, perceived self-efficacy influences and interacts with the gifted student's analytical thinking and motivates goal-setting. As a result, she is more able to remain task-committed to visualized, goal-oriented success. Each accomplishment verifies her perception of competence, which in turn increases incentive and guides her future actions. The entire process aids in the development of self-efficacy beliefs and enhances her interest in activities through the satisfaction she receives upon mastering a task (Bandura, 1986, 1995). An example is Marina, a Hispanic young woman from urban Los Angeles. While a student in an early college entrance program three thousand miles from home, she told me how she gained new insights into her Self, her abilities, and her goals. This growth came as a result of her participation in an intellectual environment that stimulated her thinking. She benefited from a new perspective of possibilities that differed substantially from the perspective of her high school environment.

Efficacy and the Learning Environment

The degree to which the gifted young female perceives herself efficacious is influenced by her learning context. Academic settings that communicate belief in able females and support their efforts strengthen personal efficacy. Studying among competent peers is a positive factor for gifted females in developing a stronger sense of efficacy. In the words of an early college entrance student, "I think just being surrounded by so many people who are intelligent [helps]. I guess it makes me feel more intelligent; and I can work harder, and I can do better."

Noble and Smyth (1995) studied female students enrolled in an early college entrance program. They reported that the majority experienced an increase in confidence in their intellectual and social skills in the challenging environment. Kem and Navan (2006) conducted focus group interviews with university honors program students. The participants reported that they felt more challenged, and therefore more capable, in honors classes than in mixed ability university courses where there were lower levels of academic demand and motivation. A recent study of self-efficacy and goal-setting at an urban university in the Southwest with a high Hispanic enrollment found that students with high self-efficacy and in good academic standing were more inclined to adapt higher level goals. The reverse was the case for students in low academic standing (Hsieh, Sullivan & Guerra, 2007). The studies all indicate that educational settings and performance significantly influence self-perceptions. The message to educators is that we enable success when we:

- Acknowledge gifted students' abilities.
- Set challenging goals for their learning.
- Provide appropriate support as they pursue those goals.

Efficacy and Future Success

There have been a number of studies examining factors that contributed to the development of successful adults. For example, one study analyzed data from the original and subsequent studies of 1500 gifted children identified by Lewis Terman—developer of the Stanford-Binet IQ test—in the 1920s. Englert and Tomlinson-Keasey (1987) found the highest correlation was between children's self-esteem, along with their motivation to achieve, and their self-efficacy and competence as adults. The higher their self-esteem and motivation as children, the more capable they were and felt as adults. The literature underscores the need for assisting personal growth and developing autonomy as important factors in career and lifestyle integration (Kerr, 1994).

Promoting Self-Efficacy in the Classroom

The importance of understanding how different educational contexts and practices affect efficacy in our learners is clear. Parents and educators as partners can assist gifted girls by providing appropriate learning environments that ensure success. There are a number of classroom practices that are effective in promoting efficacy. As is the case with many of the interventions presented in this book, teachers can implement efficacy accommodations in their classrooms without the need of acquiring costly programs or materials. My own experiences as a classroom teacher for almost three decades taught me that student development and success are not achieved through expensive programs with catchy names or "flavor of the month" professional development sessions. Rather, teachers become effective practitioners through applying, reflecting on, and internalizing the best practices that research and application affirm.

Several educational accommodations that assist students in forming strong perceptions of their ability appeared in preceding chapters. They are relevant and effective to efficacy formation because they address the individual student, adapt the learning setting to meet specific needs of individual students, and provide specific strategies that challenge and support the gifted learner. Some of the educational understandings and accommodations which affect students' perceptions of efficacy that we have examined thus far are listed on page 73.

Educational Practices that Support the Development of Self-Efficacy

- The appropriate identification of gifted students. Many unidentified gifted students who learned about giftedness as adults report that they felt *weird* and stupid. Furthermore, without identification, students do not qualify for or receive services.
- A thorough understanding of the whole child. Who is the gifted child intellectually, emotionally, and socially? Without this understanding, schools may be too quick to mislabel students who have overexcitabilities or other qualities of giftedness as having disorders (e.g., obsessive/compulsive, Asperger syndrome, ADHD).
- A willingness to respond to the types of needs that the child with overexcitabilities may have. For example, arranging an area of the room with soft lighting, monitoring noise level in the room, or providing sound-reducing ear devices.
- The promotion of self-regulated learning in the classroom. Allowing gifted students to control learning experiences in which they set learning goals, manage their time and organize resources facilitates the improvement of self-efficacy beliefs.
- Use of connected teaching, collaborative learning, and cluster grouping. These models allow for students to regulate learning and to construct knowledge through individual decision making and problem solving.
- Reflective reading and biographies give students early role models and mentors in books that have successful girls, adolescents and women as central characters. When girls see accomplished females with abilities like their own, they are able to form projected images of themselves as successful young women.
- Activities that teach successful coping and develop proactive resilience give students a sense of inner strength and ability to face difficulties productively.
- Nurturing autonomy by allowing students to develop awareness of themselves as individuals and as highly capable learners permits them to tap into their inner voice and encourages self-knowledge and self-management.

Ellis (1993) proposes other classroom dispositions that will encourage giftedness in the classroom including:

- Fostering self-expression.
- Integrating special interests into assignments.
- Dispelling gender myths.
- Encouraging dialogue between male and female students.
- Flexible gender and mixed-gender small groups.

Additional Effective Practices

A number of years ago, I interviewed a group of gifted public high school girls about their perceptions of efficacy and what factors in their learning environment influenced their perceptions (Navan, 2002a). When I asked them, "In what ways do you feel capable in your learning environment?" one girl responded that she felt strong self-efficacy in math. Her response startled me and led me to question why this would be so, in contrast with much of the research literature. All of the girls chimed it with statements like, "I could do it for hours!" or, "I could fill pages and pages working just one problem," and, "And when I finish, it's pretty!" Listening to the students, I kept asking myself, *what is the source of these feelings?* I asked the students, "What factors in the learning environment influence your feelings of being able in mathematics?" The students talked about how they liked the teacher, Mrs. V.; she was fair, and it was the one class that most of them attended together. Although helpful, their responses did not give me the detail and depth necessary to understand their reactions. I wondered if a visit to the class would increase my understanding of the classroom and help me to probe deeper into what dynamics of the teacher and the classroom setting were giving the girls such a strong sense of efficacy. The gifted resource teacher in the school arranged the visit.

Observing the girls in their 11th grade mathematics class, I noted the teacher's use of effective instructional strategies that challenged her students to excel, and the positive classroom climate she had created that provided the support they needed. For instance, before beginning the lesson, she posted and announced the learning objectives of the lesson, and then introduced the new learning by linking it to students' previous knowledge. Teaching the new material, she *guided* them through questioning to discover the concept and operations, rather than lecturing them. She then allowed time for the students to reflect on what they had just learned, pausing to allow the students to ask questions and checking for understanding before they proceeded to apply the new operations individually. In short, it was a model lesson.

The most revealing elements of the lesson—and a large part of why the gifted young women felt so capable—were those that the teacher used to create an environment in which students felt safe and assured in their learning. There was much caregiving on the part of the teacher. Students were seated in pairs, and they began the class by reviewing the homework assignment with their partner. Each of the pairs of students had been assigned one of their practice problems to solve together. Mrs. V. went from pair to pair, checking their work and offering comments and praise. I noticed that she made personal contact with each student either by commenting on a basketball game, band concert, or some other extracurricular event in which the student might be involved. If she had no information regarding a particular student, she would offer a pat on the back for a job well done with a problem or would ask for the student to tell how he or she felt about a part of the assignment.

When the lesson began, Mrs V told the class, "Today we are going to learn how to perform a new operation with *our* calculators." I emphasize the first person plural, because this is the voice she used many times in the course of the lesson. She began to elicit the content and the new mathematical operations from the students through questioning (e.g., *What do we do now? What does that tell us?*). Throughout the process of discovery and applied problem solving the students collaborated with her and constructed new knowledge. In effect, she merged her role as teacher into the role of co-participant in the learning process.

The above vignette demonstrates several effective practices that positively influence student perceptions of efficacy. The instructor became a conductor, orchestrating an ensemble that provided point and counterpoint as the class merged into pairs or collaborative groups, with solo performances as well. In effect, the interventions as described below blended together to form a community of learners.

- All participants were goal-directed with well-defined objectives.
- Communication was both professional and interpersonal, thus it both challenged and reassured the learners.
- Grouping was flexible, transitioning from pairs, to whole group, to individual student, and back.
- The teacher was a collaborator in the learning process.
- Instruction was varied and included direct instruction, paired problem solving, collaborative discovery, checking for understanding, and independent practice.

Leaving Mrs. V.'s classroom, I realized why the students felt so highly capable in such a warm and supportive environment. She was a role model, a mentor, a guide, and an example of a highly motivated mathematician and educator.

Reflective Research in the Classroom

1. In order to assist our students in developing efficacy, it is vital that we are aware of our own perceptions of efficacy, reflect on ways that we can improve any needs we have in this regard, and model efficacy in the classroom.

2. Benefits of efficacy include feeling capable in the intellectual, emotional, and behavioral areas of our lives.

3. Reflecting on the questions below, assess your strengths and needs in terms of your perceptions of your abilities.

   • Do you perceive yourself as a learner who can master and apply information effectively?

   • Do you believe yourself capable of understanding and moderating your emotional responses?

   • Do you feel capable of acting in a manner that is consistent with who you are in a variety of contexts?

4. What are your true perceptions and abilities in this regard? What reflective decisions result from your reflecting? Do you need to think more highly of your abilities? Are there areas you want to improve upon?

5. As a result of this reflection, what personal goals will you set and/or what actions will you take?

8

Agency
The Destination

Katie's Voice

Katie was assessed at five years old as a profoundly gifted student. Her parents told me at the time that they were prepared to do anything and to sacrifice anything in order to assist in the healthy development of their daughter and her gifts. That was the beginning of an extraordinary journey with an amazing young girl. Because of her unique intellectual abilities, we discovered that Katie was a candidate for radical acceleration—a term that means skipping two or more grades. For example, she completed kindergarten, first and second grade in her first year in school. She also completed middle school in less than a year of homeschooling and was enrolled simultaneously in high school and the local community college for her last few years of public schooling. Each time Katie, her parents, and I talked about her need to accelerate another grade or more, I was concerned that we not push her development too fast and risk her well-being. Each time Katie and I talked in depth in this regard, she was firm in her belief that she was ready. The school community, her parents, and I worked as a team to monitor her adjustment. Katie proved herself each time! She is currently a healthy and balanced young adult, ready to take on the world.

A parent of a profoundly gifted student in Spain, whose son experienced similar development, helped to ease my concerns about Katie's rapid acceleration when he explained how they had experienced similar issues with their son's acceleration. Their conclusions were, as he explained, like the Spanish expression that tells about how some horses do not pull the carriage. Rather, the carriage pushes them. Katie and their son are the carriages that push the horses.

Katie exhibited strong self-agency at an early age. She started a recycling business with a friend when she was a preschooler and donated the money she made to charity. Shortly after the tragedy of 9/11, all the nation's school-children were asked to say the Pledge of Allegiance at a certain time on a certain day. School was not in session in Katie's district that day, but at precisely the right hour, she went to the checkout counter of the toy store where she and her mother were shopping and asked for permission to lead the children in the store in reciting the pledge over the PA system. And they did!

One of the projects Katie and I did together while mentoring her was to study art history. Because her parents had wonderful resources with paintings and sculptures in their home, each time we learned about a new style of painting Katie would search through her house to find a representative piece from that era. In setting up the experience, I told her that for her culminating project she would act as a docent in an art gallery and give her family a tour of the art, explaining the significance of each piece. It wasn't long before Katie decided that rather than just family, she would invite members of the community and the tour would be a fundraiser for her own make-a-difference fund at the local hospital's foundation. The proceeds were to be used for the medical clinic that provided low-cost care for those without health insurance. The event raised over seven hundred dollars. Afterward, a nationally recognized art entrepreneur invited her to do the same in his local gallery.

Throughout the years, Katie demonstrated agency and impacted her environment in many ways. She ran for class president in third grade among students who were three years older than she was. She lost by only one vote. At her first high school pep rally, when students from each class were asked to volunteer and compete in a basketball shoot out to show school spirit, she was the only freshman girl to walk onto the gym floor. She took this risk even though she was several years younger than her classmates. Presently, as a young college pre-medical student, she brings stuffed animals to give to the children on her rounds of the children's wings of a research hospital; and she has already published research even though she is not yet a teenager! Through all of these experiences, Katie knows who she is and what her mission is while remaining the kind and sensitive individual that she has always been.

Emerging Self-Agency

The gifted young woman who successfully cultivates and nurtures the constructs addressed in this book—voice, resilience, autonomy and efficacy—is poised for the emergence of agency. Agency for the successful woman signifies a sense of herself as a significant participant in a society that needs her gifts. Agency is the destination. This chapter explores the construct of self-agency with the purpose of demonstrating ways in which gifted young women tap into and apply personal agency.

I can do anything I put my heart into.

—LAYKESHA

Instrumentality (i.e., operating in and impacting one's environment) and interpersonal ease characterize the concept of agency (Sollberg, Good, Fischer, Brown, & Nord, 1995). The individual who demonstrates capable human agency has learned to be self-protective, self-assertive and self-efficacious (Hawkins, 1983). Detailed below are personal skills and dispositions that contribute to the development of agency.

Aspects of Agency in Females

- **Instrumentality:** The individual possesses specific personal skills that can be applied to individual and collective problem solving.
- **Interpersonal ease:** The individual realizes her potential to impact her world. This can lead to an increase in self-confidence and the ability to interact effectively with others.
- **Self-efficacious:** The individual has developed the positive attributes of efficacy (e.g., motivation, goal-setting, mastery).
- **Self-assertive:** With increased reflective and analytical skills gained from efficacy development, the individual has the strength to defend her ideas and actions.
- **Self-protective:** In order to be an effective agent in society, the individual is aware of and respects personal needs and limits.

Adapted from Sollberg, Good, Fischer, Brown, & Nord (1995), and Hawkins (1983).

We have noted earlier that gifted female students in an early college entrance environment displayed early self-agency and that it reinforced their feelings of efficacy. They spoke of asserting themselves and their needs by attending college early, often without support or understanding on the part of their family members, their friends, or school personnel. They described creating a place where they could develop their abilities within a supportive network of friends and school staff. The young university students demonstrated personal instrumentality (using their gifts to influence and change their learning setting) in the high quality of their participation in classes and their other activities at the school. In fact, the headmaster of one early entrance academy told me how the university was modifying the undergraduate program beyond the first-year program in response to the impact of the early entrants on scholarship and academic excellence throughout the institution. Emergent self-agency builds self-efficacy, and self-agency, predictably, will become the core around which other constructs (e.g., voice, resilience, autonomy) are clustered. Through experience, this phenomenon will evolve into strong self-agency, as displayed in the lives of eminent women (Leroux, 1998; Leroux & Navan, 1998).

In more traditional learning environments, the construct of self-agency is not as evident. Students in those settings indicated their belief in their academic abilities, but any early self-agency they might possess was not yet apparent. While students in traditional settings related their abilities as learners, they did not speak of themselves as agents that affected and had the potential to affect the more extensive community environment. Indeed, the gifted resource teacher in a rural public high school shared that most of the gifted girls set college goals lower than their ability indicated. Many chose to attend two-year community colleges rather than more rigorous university environments. The message to high schools is that, by addressing the needs of gifted students through challenging and interpersonal courses, we set students up for success in college and beyond.

Agency Skills and Strategies

Bandura (2001) lists four characteristics that are central to developing agency. They are:

- Intentionality
- Forethought
- Self-reactiveness
- Self-reflectiveness

An exploration of these features as they relate to the gifted female will assist in developing educational interventions that will enhance agency development in highly able females and other students.

Intentionality

Intentionality is reflected in a commitment to a plan to carry out an action (Bandura, 2001). The intention and ability to plan actions for a purpose is key to agency in the gifted female. Rather than being a passive receiver of the actions of others, self-agency gives her the ability to develop and carry out intentions that impact her life and her society. A fundamental part of developing intentionality is effective planning. Educators who want to assist students to become active players in their environment will help students to develop efficient planning skills. For example, a teacher could demonstrate a planning cycle that consists of the elements below and then model it.

- Setting a goal.
- Reflecting on the goal.
- Adjusting and refining the goal.
- Revising and/or setting a new goal.

Students could practice setting personal and learning goals and using the planning cycle procedure as outlined above. The teacher may also post a visual of the cycle in the classroom and encourage students to refer to it in future planning. This will assist students in becoming reflective thinkers who develop the mental habit of realizing that a first thought or impulse regarding an intention is not always the best or the only possible response.

Forethought

In addition to intentional planning, agency involves forward thinking and conscious understanding of the effects of planning and action (Bandura, 2001). The ability to envision outcomes enhances the gifted female's ability to organize and modify her present condition in order to achieve her desired goals. This self-directed behavior is an outgrowth of goal-setting and forethought. Two best practices in education that will engage students in intentional planning and forethought are problem-based learning and authentic problem solving. As an early college entrance student said, "It [problem-based learning] puts it right there in front of you and you can grab hold of it, and it will always be there for you. You can always come back to that experience and say, 'OK, I know how do to this. NO problem!'"

Problem-based learning (Stepien & Gallagher, 1993) is an ideal method for facilitating the development of intentional planning and forethought through problem solving. With the problem-based learning method, students learn to define a problem clearly, develop a number of hypotheses, gather and evaluate data, modify hypotheses as needed, and develop solutions. The benefits of problem-based learning are many. Students who are agents in terms of their learning develop critical thinking skills; practice leadership skills; collaborate with their team members; and learn to access, manage, and evaluate resources.

Authentic problem solving is related to problem-based learning, but extends the concept to allow students to work in authentic settings as practicing professionals. For example, a middle school life science teacher arranges for students to take water samples at different points along the river that runs through the community. Students collect the samples and analyze them. Based on their findings, they conclude that there must be a pollution source at one point that is affecting the water quality downstream. They report their findings to the appropriate community agency, which invites the students to collaborate in further investigation.

Students who engage in authentic problem solving can impact their community in positive ways and therefore have the opportunity to view themselves as effective agents in society. In addition, working as practicing professionals in the community, they are able to see how their learning is applied in different careers and can make better-informed career decisions. There are many resources for problem-based learning and authentic problem solving, some of which are included in the Chapter 10 resources.

Best Practice Strategies for Promoting Student Agency

- Intentional planning
- Problem-based learning
- Authentic problem solving
- Collaborating in classroom management
- Creating a framework of standards
- Teaching reflective practices

Self-Reactiveness

A third aspect of agency is that of self-reactiveness, which Bandura (2001) explains as consisting of three subfunctions: self-monitoring, self-guidance, and self-reactions. A gifted female who practices a self-reactive disposition assesses her goals and actions by monitoring how they respond to her personal standards and developing a value system. Her standards guide her decision making and allow her to evaluate and modify goals and react accordingly.

In order to prepare students to self-monitor, self-guide, and self-react within a framework of standards and values, students need assistance in clarifying their personal belief system. From an early age, teachers can assist students in weaving a well-defined fabric of personal standards. A great strategy for achieving such standards is by allowing students from an early age to collaborate in developing classroom rules. Teachers and students accomplish this by discussing why learning communities need rules. Students volunteer ideas and collaboratively decide which rules should be included in the list. Students should have a say in what the consequences should be for breaking rules. It is good practice for the list of rules to be short, with clear consequences, and with fair application of the consequences. The teacher can use this activity to stress self-regulation strategies that will help the students meet the expectations that they have set for themselves.

An activity for guiding students in developing their personal standards is to ask them to think about and write down the names of people they admire. Students are asked to reflect on why they admire these individuals and what personal qualities each person has that account for the student's admiration. Students then list all the qualities they discover in role models. They should decide which qualities are actual character-based qualities and which are more superficial (e.g., wardrobe, car). Those non character-based aspects are eliminated from the list. Finally, the students decide which attributes that they find in their heroes are qualities that they want to aspire to as well. They list those in their journals and over time they add details about the qualities that they discover in themselves (e.g., *Integrity*—"I did my own work on the Science Fair project.").

Self-Reflectiveness

The fourth attribute of self-agency is that of self-reflectiveness (Bandura, 2001). Students who have developed this ability are adept in metacognitive thinking and are able to assess themselves, reflect on their motivations, and evaluate their own thinking. These skills strengthen belief in one's self-control, thus enhancing their feelings of efficacy and agency. Without these abilities, individuals would not understand why they think and solve problems effectively. Therefore, they would be unable to improve self-regulated learning. Lack of understanding of their own motivation does not allow them to take ownership of goals and set goals effectively. Finally, if they cannot evaluate their thinking, they must rely on others who do not necessarily have insight into the intricacies of their thought processes, thereby leaving them at risk of misperceptions of their efficacy.

A primary way that students learn how to reflect is through the modeling of others. A teacher has numerous opportunities to model reflection in the classroom. A recognized best practice for promoting reflective thinking is unpacking one's thinking out loud while solving a problem, while drafting a piece of writing or demonstrating a lab procedure. All are examples of reflective thinking. Teachers can also promote student reflection by pausing during discussions to ask metacognitive questions like, *How did you arrive at that conclusion?* or *Explain your thought process.* A learning log in which students write about self-generated or teacher-directed essential questions can be a valuable tool. Over the process of a unit of study, the student records his or her thinking regarding the issue so that by looking back on their thoughtful writing at the end of a unit, students can trace and understand the development of their thinking process and conceptualization.

An organization that works with high school students who are considering careers in education recently asked me to speak about giftedness to students from several local school districts. I agreed and, hoping to model best practices in the classroom for them, told them they were going to do a pre-test on the material. Before they got too nervous, I explained that this was not a test. Rather, it was a way for me to see what they knew so that they would not have to sit through material they had already learned. The pre-test consisted of only one item, which was, *Define giftedness in your own words.* Most of the students wrote very good answers. For example, "Gifted is to think, process, and reason differently than other children." Another wrote, "Having the ability and knowledge to excel among others at a faster rate." One of the responses, however, stood out and demonstrated an understanding of giftedness that hinted at the student's understanding of agency. The student wrote, "To be gifted is to *use* your knowledge and *apply* it." This high school junior had made the leap from efficacy to agency, from feeling capable to using one's abilities to change the world.

If we are to facilitate the successful development of our gifted girls, it is incumbent on us as significant adults in their lives to accompany them on their journey. From our view, we see that agency—the destination—can only be achieved through modeling and practice. They will need to learn and weave into their personal fabric the skills and dispositions of intentional planning, forethought, self-reactiveness, and self-reflection. That will prepare them for the celebration of the female spirit.

Reflective Research in the Classroom

1. Perform a climate assessment of your classroom.

2. What opportunities do students have to engage in the following best practices:

    • Effective planning?

    • Problem-based learning?

    • Authentic problem solving?

    • Shared classroom management?

    • Reflection?

3. Can you think of ways that you can integrate more of these practices into your instruction?

4. Based on your reflection, what modifications will you make in your professional practice?

9

Conclusion
A Celebration of the Female Spirit

Anna's Voice

*W*hen *I first met Anna, I was intrigued by her gentleness. She quietly listened to her classmates, taking in every word, gathering their thoughts and weaving them into an elegant synthesis. Then, in a calm, yet insistent voice, she said, "I don't think that women should feel like any of their qualities are weaknesses. It is often looked upon as women, you know, women should be soft and motherly and nurturing and caring and quiet . . . . As far as emotions go, I don't think they should be looked upon as a weakness at all. Emotions are what make us, instead of being only the scientist or only the technician, they're what make us human beings . . . I mean, through the whole discussion that's been something that we've all been talking about: that we feel good about ourselves when we feel love and when we feel other people love us also."*

The Female Spirit

An overwhelming sense of ethical grounding and a celebration of being female are vital tones that pervade the lives of successful young women. Woman becomes Self through her creativity and her authenticity (Miller, 1986). Throughout this book we see that she finds her authenticity through voice, while she is also aware that through voice she risks the abandonment and condemnation of others. Successful women are *acutely* aware of their femaleness when they see themselves as strong individuals who can nurture and sustain relationships as well. Self-in-relationship becomes a metaphor for the blending of two themes—autonomy and collaboration.

Successful women are acutely aware of their femaleness when they see themselves as strong individuals who nurture and sustain relationships.

—ANNA

Relationships

Young women achieve their awareness of Self through the strength that self-agency gives them. With strength, they realize that they are able to choose to be in relationships. They know that to sacrifice their true identity for the sake of preserving relationships means their loss of voice, thus their loss of Self. Drawing on the strength developed through efficacy and autonomy, they believe in their ability to make wise choices. The successful young women I know speak of their need to both nurture and feel nurtured by relationships. They will not let criticism of their abilities by other people deter them. They know the intellectual rejection that others may try to impose is a rejection of an essential part of who they are. They choose to be their most authentic Self.

Femaleness

Able young women emphasize their femaleness as—at the very least—equal in importance to other aspects of themselves. Anna spoke earlier of the socially perceived weakness of emotions, and her belief that the empathic caring that sprang from feelings was what gave students like her their greatest sense of efficacy. Successful girls emphasize their belief in connecting, nurturing, communicating, and interacting with others as females. They use keen social skills for creative problem solving. It was Anna who earlier said, "I think that is important [for efficacy] in feeling that you can communicate with people, touch other people, and basically relate to them."

I don't think women should feel like any of their qualities are weaknesses.

—ANNA

Capable girls are vexed when they encounter unequal treatment of
gifted females by gifted males. They are perplexed when their gifted
male classmates choose to work with other boys who are not their intellectual peers instead of choosing to work with the gifted females in their
classes. Young gifted girls express their preference for learning through
relationships—relationships with others in seminar environments, learning content through analogy, metaphor, and their individual language.

The need to connect, to withdraw, and to connect again is a theme
found throughout the literature dealing with women's development
(Gilligan, 1982; Heilbrun, 1988; Leroux & Butler-Por, 1996; Miller,
1986, 1994). Miller (1986) described it clearly when she noted that we
need to reexamine the word *autonomy*, which has different implications for women. Autonomy should not mean having to be a distinct
individual at the cost of sacrificed relationships. Our highly able
young women show that they find their femaleness in relationships
and find the strength to grow in autonomy by withdrawing into themselves and pondering the circumstances of their lives.

An important part of the environment for our gifted young women
is their private space. Melori told us earlier that she does not want others in her room without her, "because it's sacred." In order to find one's
autonomy and to reflect on Self and on one's connections, the female
learner celebrates her need to withdraw before re-entering the dance of
self-in-relationship with others. Eve, a classmate of Melori's stated, "I
think that there's a part of my conceptual framework that is about
escaping from areas. Like we are all about interaction or about doing
specific projects, but I think that some of my time is spent trying to
withdraw." Vanessa agreed, stating that, "I have to really fight for that
space in my life. I have to really think about it to find the time that it
will fit in. It's really hectic, and I think that's one of the things that make
me feel like I need that time more. When it feels like you don't have it
at all, OK, I want some of my life for a little bit of time too."

Ethical Grounding

Estés (1997) wrote of *mystery*, in the Old Spanish definition of the
word, as what we perceive in ways other than through our physical

senses. Gifted females evoke their personal encounters with an innate sense of mystery. They express the wonder of being such a small, yet complex, part of the world. An ethical grounding centers their lives. With their emotional giftedness, they grasp the many dimensions of relationships. They feel intricately woven into a universal tapestry.

Gifted young women who have navigated their path and achieved the attributes of autonomy, efficacy, and agency express a sensitivity that conveys the awe they feel about life and all it offers them. They emphasize the connectedness they feel with each other and to the world. Above all, they express their sincere commitment to make a significant contribution to their society. They are worried about themes such as world hunger, peace, global warming, and other critical global concerns. Some of our girls, as we have heard in the voices herein, have already begun to address critical global issues.

The voices of our gifted young women assist our understanding of the strengths that allow them to connect with Self *and* with others. In this way, they move beyond the knowledge received from others and construct their own personal knowledge of themselves in their world (Belenky, Clinchy, Goldberger, & Tarule, 1986). Women find Self through authenticity and their authenticity through connections. Often this quest is achieved only through strong determination, but always as a celebration of their female spirit!

Laura's Voice

Laura was a passionate artist from an early age. When she was a young child in Spain, her mother would put large pieces of butcher paper on the floor of her room and give her a brush and paints. She would create with abandon, filling sheet after sheet with marvelous creations. Her mother told me that when she painted it was as if she became a totally different child and was so consumed with her work that she was unaware of anything else in her surroundings. The conceptualization in her work was remarkable. When I visited her grandmother's house, her canvases filled the walls. There were exquisite landscapes, paintings of storms, paintings of nature, and art reflecting her conception of the mystery that lies beyond our senses. Many of these paintings were composed when she was four and five years old. Several of her pieces have been exhibited in her native Spain and throughout Europe.

Laura remembers being capable as a very young child. One day, when her sisters (who were eleven and twelve at the time) were playing chess, Laura (who was four) said that she wanted to play also. Since she had never seen chess before or learned how to play, her sisters said that she did not know how to play and told her she could not. She watched them play for about five minutes and insisted that she wanted to play. Her mother told the older girls to let her try, thinking that since she would not be able to play she would understand why she could not be a part of her sisters' game. All were astounded when Laura began to play, using the correct moves and strategies!

When Laura was a high school student, she visited the United States with a group of gifted Spanish students and took part in a summer enrichment program with gifted American students. I noticed that she was extremely shy, sensitive, and soft-spoken. Nevertheless, her gifted peers demonstrated a high degree of respect for her opinions and advice. During her second summer in the program, Laura had the opportunity to tour the university's art facilities and was enthralled with the resources that were available for students. She made up her mind that she wanted to study there. A year later, she was admitted and received a four-year international scholarship.

Laura and I kept in touch during her college years, and it was a delight to witness her development and success. She was a courageous young woman because, despite her shy nature and her very close attachment to her family—and her mother in particular—she chose to continue her development as an artist in what she felt was the best environment for her gifts. During her first year, she was extremely homesick. She acquired a small studio on campus from her art instructor and threw herself into the creative process. The act of creation became her emotional outlet, just as it had been for her as a sensitive and highly imaginative child. As her first year at the university progressed, I noticed that students would greet her spontaneously on campus, some would invite her to their family homes on weekends, and she began forming a circle of friends in the new environment.

Her second year in the university was extremely stressful for Laura because her parents and her sisters in Spain were all seriously ill with different health issues. Hers is an extremely close-knit family and, even though everyone urged her to return to the university, it was quite painful for her to do so. Drawing on all her resilience, she returned to school and managed to address her studies, despite the constant concern for her loved ones. She continued to do well with her classes and her friendships deepened. By the end of the year, she told me that although she very much wanted to return to spend the summer with her family, she also felt that she was becoming very attached to the university community. She felt as if she had a second family in the professors and students who expressed their belief in her and emotionally supported her.

Laura continued to bloom in the university environment during her junior year. She developed more friendships and took on several leadership roles within the international student program and her residential college. She exhibited some of her art in a small, nearby city, and traveled to different

American cities to visit the art museums and other attractions. Toward the end of the year Laura was asked to be a residential advisor, with the responsibility of supervising several students in the residence. She served in that role, was a leader in the organization for international students, and continued to grow as an artist.

Laura's life experience thus far demonstrates the path to success of the gifted female. She found her own unique voice in her creative expression. She weathered severe difficulties and developed resilience as a result. The time she spent separate from family afforded her the opportunity to develop personal autonomy. Through her affiliation and collaboration with others in the university community she gained a sense of efficacy. Today, Laura is an active agent in her university world, enriching herself and others as a fully engaged participant. She is poised to enter adulthood with the personal strengths necessary for her to set her goals high and to achieve them.

I ask Laura to envision the future that is ahead of her. She replies that, as a result of the opportunities to learn who she is and to create her own autonomous Self, "My future is myself and the world. My life is a path with rocks and adventures and it is not about success as a goal, it's the journey that matters, and success may be a consequence of the journey." Then she paraphrases a Spanish poet and says, "There is no path. We make our own path as we journey."

10

Annotated Resources

Advocacy Organizations

American Association for the Gifted (AAG)

The nation's oldest gifted advocacy organization, AAG publishes a newsletter, working papers, and other information.
www.aagc.org

National Association for Gifted Children (NAGC)

NAGC is an organization of parents, teachers, educators, community leaders, and others who work to educate the public regarding the needs of gifted children. They host national and regional conferences that provide information and professional development. Parent Day is a highlight of the annual conference, which is held in early November of each year. The day's schedule includes a keynote by an expert in parenting issues, a parent session, and then open admission into any of the general convention sessions.

NAGC publishes three excellent resources: *Gifted Child Quarterly*, *Parenting for High Potential*, and *Teaching for High Potential*. There is a link from the main page to NAGC's list of state affiliates. Educators and parents will find numerous resources and network opportunities on this Web page.
www.nagc.org

Supporting Emotional Needs of the Gifted (SENG)

SENG is a national organization that aims to address the emotional needs of the gifted. Composed of a network of educators and mental health professionals, along with parents and other advocates, its Web site is a valuable resource with articles, conference information, educational opportunities and more.
www.sengifted.org

The Association for the Gifted (TAG)

TAG is a division of the Council for Exceptional Children and offers assistance to professionals and parents. It offers various articles and other resources on its Web site and publishes the *Journal for the Education of the Gifted.*
www.cectag.org

The World Council of the Gifted

This international association is an excellent resource for those educators and parents who would like a more global view of giftedness. Some of the activities of World Council include an international exchange of ideas, research, and opportunities regarding giftedness. Members include delegates who are educational leaders in more than 38 countries. Their biennial conference is held in odd years in late July or early August.
www.world-gifted.org

Journals, Magazines, and Newsletters

Advanced Development

This is the premier journal on adult giftedness. It explores issues pertaining to the gifted with research, essays, poetry and other resources. Click on *Adult Giftedness & Journal.*
www.gifteddevelopment.com

Creative Kids: The National Voice for Kids

Creative Kids is a great magazine for children ages eight through fourteen. It contains art, stories, poetry, games and other information created for and by kids. On the menu, choose *Journals and Magazines.*
www.prufrock.com

Duke Gifted Letter

The Duke Talent Identification program publishes this free resource online for parents of gifted children. The newsletter is especially valuable for parents of middle and high school students.
www.dukegiftedletter.com

Gifted and Talented International (GTI)

Gifted and Talented International (GTI) is a peer-reviewed, international journal which covers the whole field of giftedness and creativity. It aims to provide a medium for communication between researchers and the practitioners and to foster collaborative research. The GTI is published twice annually.
www.journal.world-gifted.org

Gifted Child Quarterly

A publication of the National Association for Gifted Children and the premier journal of the organization, *Gifted Child Quarterly* publishes current research on giftedness and is the official archival journal of NAGC. On the menu, choose *Publications*.
www.nagc.org

Gifted Child Today

This is a magazine for teachers and parents that offers teaching strategies, gifted and talented program suggestions, and effective parenting ideas. On the menu, choose *Journals and Magazines*.
www.prufrock.com

Gifted Education Communicator

Published by the California Association for the Gifted, the *Communicator* is for parents and teachers of gifted children. It offers practical applications of research, strategies and parenting information. On the menu, choose *Publications*.
www.cagifted.org

Journal of Advanced Academics

Formally the *Journal of Secondary Gifted Education*, this new journal has a focus on advancing academic achievement for varied ages and groups of students. On the menu, choose *Journals and Magazines*.
www.prufrock.com

Journal for the Education of the Gifted

The *Journal for the Education of the Gifted* is a publication of the Council for Exceptional Children's TAG division (The Association for the Gifted). It is a highly respected research journal that addresses a wide variety of topics regarding the gifted. On the menu, choose *Journals and Magazines*.
www.prufrock.com

Imagine

From Johns Hopkins University, this is a magazine written for students of high potential in Grades 7–12. Articles are written both for and by students and professionals. Thematic issues on diverse topics like *Storytelling, Medicine and Robotics* provide glimpses into college and professional careers. From the menu, choose *More CTY for Gifted Students*.
www.cty.jhu.edu

Imagine Magazine

This online publication is a women's magazine with a new twist. The articles in the publication focus on inspiring readers to make a difference with articles on issues such as active democracy, the environment, and responsible consumerism.
www.imaginemagazine.net

Parenting for High Potential

Published by the National Association for Gifted Children, this is a magazine that provides useful information for parents such as parenting strategies, enrichment activities, and advice from experts in the fields of medicine and psychology. From the menu, choose *Publications*.
www.nagc.org

Roeper Review

Roeper is a premier research journal in the field of gifted education. It offers research articles and other features that explore all aspects of giftedness. From the menu, click on *Roeper Institute*.
www.roeper.org

2e Twice Exceptional Newsletter

The *2e Newsletter* is an online publication with articles and other resources aimed at promoting the understanding and effective education of the twice exceptional child. Twice exceptional children are those who are gifted and who also have learning or attention difficulties. www.2enewsletter.com

Understanding Our Gifted

Available online, this quarterly journal is written for parents, counselors, and teachers. Each issue has a particular focus on topics like parenting, identification, and the arts. www.our-gifted.com

Resources for Teachers and Parents

Annemarie Roeper Qualitative Assessment Method®

For assessments in English or Spanish, contact:
Joy L. Navan
Certified QA Practitioner
jbnavans@bellsouth.net

For a list of other QA Practitioners, contact:
Barbara Mitchell Hutton
Executive Director
Rocky Mountain School for the Gifted
5490 Spine Road
Boulder, CO 80301
blmh@rms.org

The Center for Talented Youth (CTY)

Housed at Johns Hopkins University, CTY offers a multitude of services, including distance learning, summer programs, family academic programs, and college resources. www.cty.jhu.edu

Davidson Institute

The Davidson Institute supports profoundly gifted children and their parents through a variety of initiatives, including parent networking, summer camps, and special programs. Students apply for admission to the Institute and, if approved, are eligible to participate in its offerings. www.davidsoninstitute.org

Gifted Development Center

The Gifted Development Center, directed by Dr. Linda Silverman, provides many services to gifted children and their parents. Assessment services, a speaker's bureau, and access to information about giftedness through a variety of media are examples of resources. www.gifteddevelopment.com

Hoagies Gifted Education Page

Hoagies Gifted is *the all things gifted* Web resource! Updated often, it contains links to the latest in research, resources and issues that affect gifted students. There are specific sections for Parents, Teachers and Children. Read *Gifted 101: A Guide for First Time Visitors* first. www.hoagiesgifted.org

Institute for Educational Advancement

The Institute for Educational Advancement is an organization that provides services for gifted student in the form of special camps, consultation and counseling, and apprenticeships in universities and research environments. www.educationaladvancement.org

The Templeton National Report on Acceleration

A Nation Deceived: How Schools Hold Back America's Brightest Students is a study, founded by the Templeton Foundation, that reviews fifty years of past and current research regarding acceleration. Contrary to common beliefs, acceleration—when planned and implemented appropriately—is good practice and students report positive benefits when looking back on the experience. www.nationdeceived.org

National Society for the Gifted and Talented

Students who qualify for membership in this organization receive information regarding programs and services that address their needs. Additionally, students receive pertinent information to assist

with enrichment and educational planning. Parents have the opportunity to correspond with other parents of the gifted.
www.nsgt.org/index.asp

Homeschooling Resources

A to Z Home's Cool

This Web site contains over a thousand pages, linked to curricula, a chat room, and many other valuable resources compiled by an expert in homeschooling.
www.homeschooling.gomilpitas.com

Creative Homeschooling: A Resource Guide for Smart Families

Author Lisa Rivero provides a wealth of ideas and activities that respond to the high ability needs of gifted homeschoolers. Published by Great Potential Press.
www.giftedbooks.com

Gifted Homeschoolers Forum (GHF)

Created and directed by a group of mothers of gifted homeschoolers, GHF offers a variety of resources. Check out *Favorite Things* for student-oriented learning activities.
www.giftedhomeschoolers.org

Moving Beyond the Page

This site offers curriculum ideas and other resources for parents of gifted homeschoolers.
www.movingbeyondthepage.com

Distance Learning

Johns Hopkins Center for Talented Youth

CTYOnline has online course offerings for students as young as Grade 3 (language arts) and through high school in mathematics, language arts, and computers, among others. From the menu, click on CTYOnline-Distance Ed.
www.cty.jhu.edu

Northwestern University Center for Talent Development

CTD's Gifted Learning Links programs offers enrichment courses such as mythology and forensic evidence for Grades 3–6; honors courses like Latin, musical theater, philosophy and psychology for Grades 6–12; and AP courses for Grades 6–12.
www.ctd.northwestern.edu

Stanford University: Educational Program for Gifted Youth-Online High School

Stanford offers a three year online high school diploma for gifted students, culminating in a diploma. The goal of the program is to provide gifted students access to high quality curriculum and learning that may not be available in traditional settings.
www.epgy.stanford.edu/ohs

Virtual High School (VHS)

VHS offers online courses, including AP Courses, in several subject areas. Schools and individual students are eligible to participate in the programs.
www.govhs.org

Resource and Enrichment Web sites for Parents, Teachers, and Students

AdLit.org

This is a site for parents and teachers that has resources and classroom strategies that focus on literacy skills in Grades 4–12. Look at the *Teacher Tip* and *Parent Tip* sections.
www.adlit.org

American Museum of Natural History (AMNH)

The American Museum of Natural History online offers video podcasts of exhibits, science bulletins, professional development, and educational activities for children.
www.amnh.org

American Museum of Natural History: Ology

The AMNH Web site for kids explores disciplines like archeology, marine biology, astronomy, and more. Kids perform investigations as if they are professionals in the discipline.
www.ology.amnh.org

The Big6

Big6 is an excellent tool for helping students develop self-regulated learning skills. Students in primary, elementary, and secondary grades organize tasks and solve problems by following the steps in the model. It is especially useful with technology-based information.
www.big6.com/kids

Children's Encyclopedia of Women

Created and updated by school children in New York, this site contains information about diverse historical figures and current women of influence.
www.pocanticohills.org/womenenc/womenenc.htm

The Choices Program

The Choices Program is based at Brown University and has as its mission the engagement of students in international issues through preparation in the necessary citizenship skills. The site has links to teaching resources, professional development opportunities, and other initiatives.
www.choices.edu

Digital History

A consortium of institutions created this site which provides access to primary sources and other rich history resources. If history teachers and their students had only one site for historical research, this would be my first choice.
www.digitalhistory.uh.edu

Discovery Education: Discovery School

Intended for educators, this site contains valuable resources for the educator: lesson plans, clip art, and more.
school.discoveryeducation.com

Fathom

This is a marvelous site for online learning. It consists of a consortium of institutions that include the American Film Institute, the British Library, the British Museum, Cambridge University Press, Columbia University, London School of Economics, Natural History Museum, New York Public Library, RAND, Science Museum, University of Chicago, University of Michigan, Victoria & Albert Museum, and Woods Hole Oceanographic Institution. It includes access to thousands of pages of free access content.
www.fathom.com

Get Writing

From the BBC, this site allows budding writers to learn creative writing skills with mini-courses and audio clips by authors on topics such as developing voice and writing historical fiction.
www.bbc.co.uk/dna/getwriting

Green Architecture

For the future architect, *Architecture Week*, provides an overview of architecture initiatives that address environmental principles.
www.architectureweek.com/topics/green.html

iEARN: International Education and Resource Network

iEARN is a network that allows teachers and their students to collaborate on authentic projects with students from around the world. Learning circles form partnerships among a group of schools from different countries.
www.iearn.org

A Lifetime of Color

A Lifetime of Color is a site sponsored by Sanford Art. It teaches art concepts and principles and provides lesson plans for educators and art activities for student.
www.alifetimeofcolor.com

The Louvre

This is the official site of the Louvre. Students can view images from the permanent collection and current exhibits. Visitors may choose *English* from the homepage.
www.louvre.fr

The Metropolitan Museum of Art

The educational resource link on the museum's Web site provides access to online images and other resources.
www.metmuseum.org

Museum of Modern Art (MoMA)

The MoMA's educational page offers *Destination: Modern Art* for children, ages five through eight. For high school students, *The Red Studio* addresses questions and issues about art. *Modern Teachers Online*, provides guides, images, and lesson plans for educators.
www.moma.org/education

National Gallery of Art (NGA)

The National Gallery of Art education page allows teachers and students to search for resources by curriculum, topics and artists. Students will love the *Super-Learner Interactives* (click on *NGA Kids*), where the child becomes the artist.
www.nga.gov/education

National Museum of Women in the Arts

Located in Washington, D.C. there is a link on the Web site to educational resources, many of which are available online.
www.nmwa.org

National Science Digital Library (NSDL)

NSDL has resources and information for educators of K–12 students. Through a partnership with the National Science Teachers Association, the site offers links to professional development seminars for teachers.
www.nsdl.org

National Women's Hall of Fame

An excellent resource for young girls, this site contains links to the biographies of hundreds of women, inductees into the Hall.
www.greatwomen.org

The New York Philharmonic

On the homepage of the New York Philharmonic Orchestra, click on *Kidzone* for an interactive educational resource.
www.nyphil.org/education

PBS Teachers Page

This Public Broadcasting Service Web site offers educational activities and professional development, content resources, and more.
www.pbs.org/teachers

PhysLink: Physics and Astronomy Online

This is a great site for students (and their teachers) with questions and an interest in physics and astronomy.
www.physlink.com

The Prado Museum

Located in Madrid, Spain, educators and students have access to selected images of the collection, one of the finest in the world. This page has links to many other Spanish Culture resources.
www.spanisharts.com

Problem-Based Learning (PBL)

The link below is to the Problem-Based Learning page on the educational page of the program *Nature*, from the Public Broadcasting Service. It gives an overview of PBL and also links to lessons and other educational resources.
www.pbs.org/wnet/nature/teach.html

San Francisco Symphony Kids

SFS Kids is a great music resource site that teaches students the sights and sounds of the orchestra, allows them to learn the elements of music and gives them the chance to create their own musical compositions. www.sfskids.org

Smithsonian Education

The site is a virtual site for accessing many of the Smithsonian's diverse museums and resources. Teachers and their students can explore science, art, history, and people and places online. www.smithsonianeducation.org

Washington State University World Civilization Page

This site links teachers and students to online resources that explore world cultures. There is an area of general resources that provides access to online maps and museums, among other resources. Specific links to diverse cultures explore cultural resources in art, history, philosophy, and other scholarly disciplines. www.wsu.edu/~dee/WORLD.HTM

Webquests

Webquests engage students in Web-based inquiry learning and is an excellent modification for gifted students. www.webquest.org

Women's History

Below is a link to About.com's resource page. It contains links to history, biographies, and other resources. www.womenshistory.about.com

Women in History

This site contains links to the biographies of women, historical figures in our history. www.lkwdpl.org/WIHOHIO/figures.htm

Book Recommendations for Gifted Females

Grades K–3

Anholt, Laurence. *Stone Girl, Bone Girl: The Story of Mary Anning* **(Illustrated by Sheila Moxley). Orchard Books, 1999.**
For the budding archeologist or paleontologist, this book tells the story of Mary Anning, a fossil hunter in the 19th century who discovered a skeleton of an ichthyosaur from 165 million years ago. With beautiful illustrations, the reader learns of Anning's rage to know, her development as a fossil hunter, and the importance of *role models* and *mentoring*.

Dorros, Arthur. *Abuela* **(Illustrated by Elisa Kleven). Dutton Children's Books, 1991.**
In an imaginative and beautifully illustrated tale, a young Hispanic girl visits different places in the American city where she lives. Through connections with her extended family, she discovers *voice*, *connections* and *affiliation*.

Giovanni, Nikki. *Rosa* **(Illustrated by Bryan Collier). Henry Holt and Company, 2005.**
This is the biography of the *resilient* and *ethically grounded* Rosa Parks. It is a Caldecott Honor book.

Goble, Paul. *The Girl Who Loved Wild Horses.* **Atheneum Books for Young Readers, 2001.**
This book is a Caldecott Medal winner, awarded annually for the most distinguished American picture book for children. It is the story of a Native American girl whose love for horses is a gift that is recognized by her people. In the end, her *gifts* and her *autonomy* are affirmed by her parents, and she is given the freedom to pursue her own path.

Sendak, Maurice. *Outside Over There.* **Harper Trophy, 1989.**
This is the story of Ida, whose father is away at sea and whose mother sits, waiting, in the arbor. Ida cares for and rescues her baby sister, demonstrating *agency* and *resilience*. This book may be too intense for young gifted children with imaginational or emotional overexcitabilities.

Thomas, Joyce Carol. *Brown Honey in Broomwheat Tea* **(Illustrated by Floyd Cooper). HarperCollins, 1993.**
This beautifully written and illustrated collection of poems celebrates heritage and identity of the African American young girl. It sings of *autonomy*, *efficacy*, *affiliation*, and *resilience*. The book is an award winner of a Coretta Scott King Non-Violent Social Change honor.

Grades 4–5

Brink, Carol Ryrie. *Caddie Woodlawn.* **Simon & Schuster, 1973.**
Based on the life of the author's grandmother, the book recounts a year in the life of the main character, Caddie, and her pioneer family in the 1860s. Caddie prefers being outdoors with her brothers, rather than learning the more ladylike style of the indoors. Affirmed in her preference by her father, who believes she needs to be strong to endure the difficult life of the northern prairie, Caddie's adventures illustrate her authentic *voice, autonomy,* and *resilience.* A Newbery Medal winner.

Byars, Betsy. *The Summer of the Swans* **(Illustrated by Ted CoConis). Puffin Books, 1996.**
Sara is fourteen and at an awkward stage of adolescence, not understanding her body, her family, nor life. When her younger brother disappears, she forgets about herself and in the process finds herself, her *autonomy,* and her need for *affiliation,* at the same time. A Newbery Medal winner.

Greene, Bette. *Philip Hall Likes Me. I Reckon Maybe.* **Dell, 1974.**
Beth Lambert is an African American girl of eleven, growing up in a small town in Arkansas. She likes Philip, who she considers the cutest and the smartest boy in school. Because she likes him, she realizes that she might let him be best so that he will like her too. Beth has to make a choice between going to college and losing the friendship of Philip when she realizes the importance of her dream to become a veterinarian. She chooses *voice, authenticity,* and *efficacy.*

Gerson, Mary-Joan. *Fiesta Femenina: Celebrating Women in Mexican Culture* **(Illustrated by Maya Christina Gonzalez). Barefoot Books, 2001.**
Gerson retells folktales from Mayan, Aztec, and other Mexican cultures, whose main characters demonstrate their gifts of intelligence and their strength. The illustrations are especially rich and add to the cultural value for students.

L'Engle, Madeleine. *A Wrinkle in Time.* **Farrar, Straus and Giroux, 1962.**
Meg Murry is the only daughter of four children in a fascinating family. Her parents are eminent scientists and all of the children are gifted. Their adventures take them to unknown worlds. Meg's journey is also within herself, where she finds her *agency* and her *autonomy.* The other books in L'Engle's *The Time Quartet,* are just as valuable. A Newbery Medal winner.

Levine, Gail Carson. *Ella Enchanted.* **Harper Trophy, 1997.**
Ella was given a curse at birth that obliged her to obey any command. She learns of the curse at age fifteen from her dying mother. Warned by her mother never to reveal the secret of the curse, Ella resolves to find the fairy who gave her the gift of obedience. In the process, she finds her own strong will and *autonomy*. A Newbery Honor book.

Lowry, Lois. *Anastasia Krupnik.* **Yearling, 1979.**
Anastasia is ten and is at a point in her life when nothing seems right. She has a teacher that does not understand her poetic license. The boy she has a crush on seems to ignore her, and her parents are having another baby. Her secret green notebook becomes the place where she sorts out her life with lists, and comes to understand herself as well.

Montgomery, L.M. *Anne of Green Gables.* **HarperCollins, 1998.**
This classic series about the adventures, adolescence, and coming of age of the orphan Anne Shirley, is a must-read for gifted girls. Arriving on Prince Edward Island as an eleven-year-old, Anne's guardians are middle-aged brother and sister farmers who expected a boy to help with chores. It is not long before Anne has charmed their hearts and those of the entire community. Anne is lively and *gifted* with a strong sense of *self*. With the development of *voice, resilience, efficacy,* and *autonomy* throughout the series she provides a strong role model for girls during adolescence. Other books in the series are: *Anne of the Island, Anne of Windy Poplars, Anne's House of Dreams, Anne of Ingleside,* and *Anne of Avonlea.*

Patron, Susan. *The Higher Power of Lucky* **(Illustrated by Matt Phelan). Atheneum Books for Young Readers, 2006.**
A Newbery Medal winner, this book tells the story of ten-year-old Lucky. Lucky is smart and resourceful, with a thirst for learning. She fears her guardian may abandon her and return to France, leaving Lucky to be sent to an orphanage. She believes that her *higher power* is the answer to her concerns. In searching for it, she finds her *resilience* and her *efficacy*.

Speare, Elizabeth George. *The Witch of Blackbird Pond* **(Illustrated by Barry Moser). Houghton Mifflin Illustrated American Classics, 1986.**
Kit, an orphan girl of sixteen, leaves Barbados to sail to the Connecticut Colony, where she will live with her maternal aunt. Wanting to be accepted and loved in her new land, she finds her *voice* endangered in the midst of a closed, puritanical society. With *resilience* and *efficacy*, she stands her ground and finds her *authenticity*. Winner of the Newbery Medal for significant contribution to American literature for children.

Grades 6–8

Creech, Sharon. *Walk Two Moons.* **HarperCollins, 1994.**
A Newbery Medal winner, this is the story of the odyssey of self-discovery of an early adolescent Native American girl, who—on the journey in search of her mother—discovers her own authentic *voice.*

Fenner, Carol. *Yolonda's Genius.* **Margaret K. McElderry Books, 1995.**
Yolonda, an African America girl, is a fifth grader whose mother, a widow, has recently moved with Yolanda and her little brother from Chicago to Michigan in an attempt to find a safer environment for them. Yolanda considers herself a Chicago girl. She is big and strong—both physically and mentally—and is not easily adapting to the small town feel of Grand River. Her little brother, Andrew, is in first grade and is having trouble learning to read. He is a quiet, sensitive boy and rarely talks; but Yolanda is convinced that he is a musical genius and makes it her mission to prove this. In the end, it is his big sister's genius, along with her *voice, resilience,* and *agency* that introduces Andrew's genius to the world. A Newbery Honor Book.

Keller, Helen. *The Story of My Life.* **Random House, 2004.**
The amazing biography of a remarkable American heroine traces her development of *efficacy* and her impact on the world (*agency*).

Krull, Kathleen. *Lives of Extraordinary Women: Rulers, Rebels (and What the Neighbors Thought)* **(Illustrated by Kathryn Hewitt). Harcourt Children's Books, 2000.**
With a playful pen, the author tells the stories of strength, *autonomy, agency,* and *resilience* of twenty historical and highly influential women, including Harriet Tubman, Eleanor Roosevelt, Wilma Mankiller and others.

Larson, Kirby. *Hattie Big Sky.* **Delacorte Books, 2006.**
Hattie is an orphan of 16 when she leaves Iowa to homestead land that an uncle left her in Montana. In order to keep her land, she must fence and cultivate it within a year. Her struggle to do so proves her *efficacy* and her *resilience.* This is a Newbery Honor book.

Paterson, Katherine. *Jacob Have I Loved.* **HarperCollins, 1980.**
A Newbery Medal winner, this is the poignant story of Louise, an intellectually gifted child who feels unloved and different. Her twin sister, Caroline, is the favored and favorite child of the family and the community. Louise's grandmother, with poisonous words, constantly suggests that she is unwanted. It is not until she is in her teens that she proves herself in the world of the Chesapeake Bay watermen. The sense

of *efficacy* gained from work starts her on the path of finding her own *autonomy* and to creating her future as a strong and *resilient* individual.

Wilkerson, J.L. *A Doctor to Her People: Dr. Susan LaFlesche Picotte*. Acorn Books, 1999.
This book is a biography and story of the determination, *efficacy*, and *resilience* of Susan LaFlesche. The daughter of an Omaha chief, she was the first Native American woman doctor, graduating from Woman's Medical College in Philadelphia.

Grades 9–12

Budhos, Marina. *Ask Me No Questions*. Simon & Schuster Children's Publishing, 2007.
Fourteen-year-old Nadira and her family emigrated from Bangladesh and tried to become legal citizens. After September 11, 2001, one dishonest lawyer, and another who failed to get them permanent papers, they try to seek entry into Canada. When her father is detained at the border, her mother and sister are helpless to do anything. Nadira learns *agency* and *resilience* as she works to reconcile her family. An American Library Association Best Book for Young Adults.

Cole, Brock. *Celine*. Farrar, Straus and Giroux, 2003.
The author shares the story of Celine, a young artist of sixteen. Left with her stepmother while her father is traveling in Europe, she struggles with adolescent problems—the essay that she needs to complete, the neighbor's boy in her care, her relationship with her stepmother. Her hope is to finish her school year with no major problem so she can spend her summer in Italy, as promised by her father. The *efficacy* and *agency* that Celine shows in difficult situations will be helpful for gifted girls.

Fuso, Kimberly Newton. *Tending to Grace*. Laurel-Leaf Books, 2005.
Cornelia is a bright teenager with a purposeless, self-centered mother. When her mother leaves for the West with a boyfriend, Cornelia is dropped off at the rural New England home of Agatha, her great aunt. Niece and aunt discover through each other much about their pain and the barriers they have constructed. Cornelia discovers and strengthens her true inner *voice*, despite the outward silence she maintains because of her stuttering. An ALA Best Book for Young Adults.

Lasky, Kathryn. *Beyond the Burning Time*. Scholastic Books, 1996.
This is the story of the intelligent and strong Mary Chase and her family in Salem Town, Massachusetts. The story takes place during

the late 17th century Pilgrims' paranoia about witchcraft. It is a Newbery Honor book.

Rosoff, Meg. *How I Live Now*. **Random House Children's Books, 2006.** Troubled fifteen-year-old Daisy travels from New York to England, sent by her father and stepmother to visit an aunt and cousins. She quickly bonds with her Aunt Penn and four cousins. Penn leaves the country on a peace mission and shortly thereafter England is attacked and invaded. Troops eventually take over her cousin's farm, separate the boys from the girls and send them away. Daisy must use her cunning and *resilience* in fighting to survive and to protect her nine-year-old cousin, Piper. An ALA Best Book for Young Adults.

Sayres, Meghan Nuttall. *Anahita's Woven Riddle*. **Harry N. Abrams, 2006.**
Anahita fights for her *autonomy* against her Persian culture's tradition that gives her parents the authority to arrange her marriage. She persuades her father to allow her to weave a riddle into her wedding carpet that any potential suitor must unravel in order to have her in marriage. In the end her determination allows for her to be rewarded her *yar*, her chosen one. An ALA Best Book for Young Adults.

Appendix A

The Voices: Participants on the Journey

Anna

Anna was an early college entrance student; a slender and gentle young woman who spoke softly and hesitantly, yet very articulately, as she painted her self-picture with verbal images and metaphors. Her first language was Lithuanian and she reports that her first recollection of being bright was when she was given a spelling test in kindergarten and wrote *stag* under the picture instead of *deer* because the animal had antlers.

Beth

Beth was an amiable and expressive member of the gifted program and a twelfth grader at a small public high school in the Northeast. She recalled becoming aware of being bright when she was in fourth grade. Though a strong student, Beth expressed frustration about not being organized in terms of her study skills.

Brenda

Brenda was an eleventh grade gifted student in a small, rural public high school. She was first aware that she was capable when she was accelerated in Math in second grade. Her enrichment coordinator described her as having a *natural giftedness*.

Brigid

Brigid was an exceptionally gifted middle school student who demonstrated strong gifted intensities and sensitivities. A brilliant artist, she also had strong abilities in mathematics and engineering.

Bridget

Bridget was an eleventh grade gifted student at a small public high school. She had an older brother whom the gifted resource teacher described as, "mentally perfect." Her sister was a talented athlete. Bridget exhibited a combination of intellectual and athletic talents plus natural leadership ability.

Cameron

Cameron grew up and attended public schools in a small southern city. A gifted musician, mathematician, and leader, she had a strong spiritual core that one sensed in all that she did through church and community service, youth leadership, and more. After high school, Cameron attended a private university of world renown in the Northeastern United States.

Caroline

Caroline was a highly creative young girl who attended a private elementary school in a small southern city. She was precocious as an artist, highly verbal, and demonstrated abilities in the dramatic arts.

Cheryl

Cheryl remembered, very early on, "everyone being amazed by my memory skills." She was a gifted high school student in a rural public high school in the eleventh grade.

Christine

Christine was an attractive, soft-spoken young woman in a public high school whose earliest recollection of being bright was of being placed in an enrichment program in elementary school.

Crystal

Crystal was a highly intuitive learner. She did not encounter academic challenge until late in her high school career. A lack of study skills and a weak sense of efficacy were barriers to her continuous learning progress.

Darcie

Darcie was in the eleventh grade at a small public high school. She also was studying early childhood education at a nearby educational cooperative. I found it interesting that—unlike other students' answers when solicited—she wrote of no early recollection of being bright. She also perceived herself as different from most of her classmates and felt that some of the teaching in school was in conflict with her strong Christian belief.

Deborah

Deborah was a first year honors student in a public university in the Southeast. She loved creating art and playing guitar and found them to be emotional outlets for her in the intense and stressful life of a pre-med student.

Elyssa

Elyssa first became aware of her abilities in second grade when she tested well and was placed in a gifted learning program. She has penetrating blue eyes that speak to her well developed intellectual giftedness. I got to know Elyssa while she was attending an early entrance to college program in the Northeast. She had five siblings and lived with foster parents, who were teachers.

Emily

Emily was a highly gifted student in a rural public high school. The oldest of two female siblings, her father had been a world class competitor in sports. Emily reflected her father's drive and perfectionism.

Eve

Eve was an eleventh grade student at a private school in the Northeast. Her demeanor and her behaviors conveyed a strong sense of self. She reported that she was aware of her abilities from an early age when her parents told her so.

Gail

Gail was a twelfth grade student in a small, rural public school district in the Northeast and from a farming family. She spoke in animated tones with vibrant facial expressions to communicate her ideas and feelings. A member of the gifted program, she remembered being accelerated in reading in elementary school.

Gwen

Gwen was an eleventh grade gifted student in the public school and an excellent student. The middle child of three siblings in her rural family, she stressed that she worked hard and listened well.

Hailey

Hailey spent her childhood in the fifties in the eastern United States and her adolescence on the West Coast. She is currently an educator and researcher in higher education.

Heidi

Heidi was a junior in a private school. She first was aware of her abilities when, "In kindergarten we talked about how we could learn things *by heart*. I realized how many songs, poems, and other things I knew and I had learned by myself."

Jackie

Petite and perky, Jackie was an eleventh grade gifted student and the only daughter of a single mother. She rarely spoke in the group of other students at a rural public high school in the Northeast. However, when she did contribute she was very expressive. Jackie remembers her grandfather teaching her to read before she started school. Jackie made it clear that she was not only concerned about academics, but that, "I strive for excellence in the athletic field as well."

Jacqueline

Jacqueline was a pretty, petite and very feminine young woman who studied in an early college entrance program. Her earliest memories of being aware of her abilities are having her artistic talent recognized at age three. She also recalls that she was placed in her school's gifted and talented program in first grade.

Jordyn

I first met Jordyn as a kindergarten student when her mother brought her for assessment. She had intense, blue eyes and one could observe that even as young as she was, she had a strong sense of efficacy and of Self.

Katherine

Katherine was a first year honors student in a public university in the Southeast. She loved the natural world and often hiked along the nearby lake, relating that this was how she found balance from her busy academic responsibilities.

Katie

Katie was a profoundly gifted early adolescent. Her deep, dark eyes and long, straight dark hair hint of her Native American heritage. She was the only biological child of her parents and had a half-brother who was several years older than she. She was first aware of her giftedness when she was "playing school" with her babysitter as a two-year-old and recognized letters and sounds.

Laura

Laura was an exceptionally gifted young woman who had already achieved international recognition for her paintings. She was the youngest of three daughters. Her Spanish father was a small business owner, and her mother was a historian.

Laykesha

Laykesha was a slight, perky, African-American early college entrance student who remembered reading, counting and doing arithmetic before entering elementary school. She was in gifted and talented programs in public school and shared that, of six living generations, hers is only the second generation to read and write.

Lilly

Lilly was an exceptionally gifted child whom I met when she was five years old. Her Russian father approached me after a presentation on overexcitabilities and said that I needed to assess his first-generation American daughter since she had all the characteristics that I described in my presentation. An accomplished pianist at a young age and a stellar student of ballet, I found Lilly to be a highly creative spirit.

Maki

Maki grew up speaking Japanese and English. An early college entrance student, she remembered being aware of her abilities in preschool in Japan where she was sent to live with her grandparents for several months. She could read Japanese at four.

Malena

Malena was an African-American student with a personality that exudes sociability. An early college entrance student, she was able to read before entering school and was identified as gifted as a second grader.

Marina

Marina was a Hispanic student from Los Angeles. I met her when she was three thousand miles from home, studying in an early college entrance program at an engineering school in the Northeast.

Maureen

Maureen was petite, vivacious, and expressive with a warm smile which flashes often. Her earliest recollection of being bright is that her parents always said so, as well as her daycare teacher. Maureen was a student in an early college entrance program and was very talented in the performing arts, especially vocal music.

Meg

Meg was a fifth grade student in a small rural public school in the Northeast. She displayed keen abilities in math and language arts and had natural leadership ability. She was the youngest child in her family that included two older brothers and whose parents were university faculty members.

Melori

Melori was an Indonesian student in her senior year in a private high school. She spoke English very well and was a warm and friendly young woman. Although not recognized as gifted in a country that did not identify for giftedness, the headmaster of the school affirmed her strong abilities.

Paz

Paz was an exceptionally gifted high school student from Spain who attended a university summer enrichment program for three years. She was a peacemaker among her friends and had all the characteristics of high emotional giftedness-sensitivity, intuitive thinking, and intensity.

Ryann

Ryann was a first year university honors program student. With a gentle demeanor she expressed her love of academics and challenge, as well as her enjoyment of playing sports. Ryann revealed a deep spiritual center and a love of the natural world.

Sarah

Sarah had long, reddish blonde hair and expressive eyes. She was a friendly, relaxed, and dedicated athlete at the early college entrance program. She remembered reading with her mom before she went to school and learning about different types of rocks. She expressed global self-efficacy when she told me, "I just have this feeling within me that I don't have to prove myself to anyone . . . I just feel capable."

Vanessa

Vanessa, tall with fine, curly long brown hair was a junior in a private school when I met her. She was the only child of her biological parents and a first generation Greek-American. An early recollection she had was as a preschooler. She knew that the family was going for I-C-E C-R-E-A-M, even though the words were spelled out by her parents.

Appendix B

Learning Log Template

PERSONAL LEARNING LOG
Name: _____ Date: _____
*Goal for the day : _____   _____ Efficacy Estimate: _____
Estimated time to complete: _____
Materials and other resources needed: 1. _____   2. _____   3. _____   4. _____   5. _____
Procedures: 1. _____   2. _____   3. _____   4. _____   5. _____
Actual Efficacy Rating: _____
*If this is a large project which will take several days, state the project and then state the segment to be completed today.   Joy L. Navan (2009)

References

Adams, C. M. (1996). Gifted girls and science: Revisiting the issues. *Journal of Secondary Gifted Education, 7*, 447–458.

Baker, J. A. (1996). Everyday stressors of academically gifted adolescents. *Journal of Secondary Gifted Education, 7*, 356–368.

Bandura, A. (1982). Self-efficacy mechanism in human agency. *American Psychologist, 37*, 122–147.

Bandura, A. (1986). *Social foundations of thought and action. A social cognitive* theory. Englewood Cliffs, NJ: Prentice Hall.

Bandura, A. (1995). *Self-efficacy in changing societies.* New York: Cambridge University Press.

Bandura, A. (1997). *Self Efficacy: The exercise of control.* New York: W.H. Freeman.

Bandura, A. (2001). Social cognitive theory: An agentic perspective. In *Annual Review of Psychology, 52*, 1–26.

Begley, S. (2007, January). How thinking can change the brain. *The Wall Street Journal.* Retrieved September 25, 2007 from http://online.wsj.com/article/SB116915058061980596.html.

Belenky, M. F., Clinchy, B. M., Goldberger, N. R., & Tarule, J. M. (1986). *Women's ways of knowing.* New York: Basic Books.

Brown, L. M., & Gilligan, C. (1992). *Meeting at the crossroads: Women's psychology and girls' development.* New York: Ballantine Books.

Csikszenmihalyi, M. (1990). *Flow: The psychology of optimal experience.* New York: Harper Perennial.

Cummings, E. E. (1994). *100 selected poems.* New York: Grove Press.

Dabrowski, K. (1972). *Psychoneurosis is not an illness.* London: Gryf.

Dixon, J. P., Hickey, M., & Dixon, J. K. (1992). A causal model of the way emotions intervene between creative intelligence and conventional skills. *New Ideas in Psychology, 10*, 233–251.

Englert, A. M., & Tomlinson-Keasey, C. (1987). Competence and self-efficacy among the gifted. *Gifted International, 4*(1), 8–13.

Estés, Clarissa Pinkola (1997). *Women who run with the wolves: Myths and stories of the wild woman archetype.* New York: Random House.

Freire, P. (1971). *Pedagogy of the oppressed.* New York: Seaview.

Fisher, H. (1999). *The first sex: The natural talents of women and how they are changing the world.* New York: Ballantine Books.

Gallos, J. (1995). Gender and silence: Implications of women's ways of knowing. *College Teaching, 43,* 101–105.

Garrison, L. (1993). Professionals of the future: Will they be female? Will they be ethnically diverse? *Roeper Review, 15,* 161–164.

Gilligan, C. (1982). *In a different voice: Psychological theory and women's development.* Cambridge, MA: Harvard University Press.

Gilligan, C. (1994). Joining the resistance: Psychology, politics, girls and women. In M.B. Berger (Ed.), *Women beyond Freud: New concepts in feminine psychology* (pp. 99–145). New York: Brunner/Mazel Publishers.

Gilligan, C., Lyons, N. P., & Hanmer, T. (1990). *Making connections: The Relational worlds of adolescent girls at Emma Willard School.* Cambridge, MA: Harvard University Press.

Harasim, L. (1991). Collaborative learning in higher education. In *Collaborative learning in higher education: Proceedings of the Teaching Conference.* Bloomington, IN: Indiana University.

Hawkins, B. (1983). Agency and communion: An alternative to masculinity and femininity. (ERIC Document Reproduction Service No. ED 243 051).

Heilbrun, C. G. (1988). *Writing a woman's life.* New York: Ballantine Books.

Hsieh, P., Sullivan, J. R., & Guerra, N. S. (2007). Closer look at college students: Self efficacy and goal orientation. *Journal of Advanced Academics, 18,* 454–476.

Kem, L., & Navan, J. L. (2006). Gifted students in college: Implications for advisors and faculty. *NACADA Journal, 26*(2), 21–28.

Kerr, B. A. (1994). *Smart girls two: A new psychology of girls, women and giftedness.* Dayton, OH: Ohio Psychology Press.

Leroux, J. A. (1994). A tapestry of values: Gifted women speak out. *Gifted Education International, 9,* 167–171.

Leroux, J. A. (1998). Follow your dream: Gifted women and the cost of success. *Gifted Education International, 13,* 4–12.

Leroux, J. A., & Butler-Por, N. (1996). Keeping faith in ourselves: A comparative study of Canadian and Israeli women's perceptions of their achievement. *Gifted and Talented International, 11,* 16–21.

Leroux, J. A., & Navan, J. L. (1998). Models and mirrors: Eminent women and gifted young women. *NAGC Research Briefs, 12.*

Lind, S. (2001). Overexcitability and the gifted. *SENG Newsletter, 1*(1), 3–6.

Lovecky, D. V. (1996). Creative connections: Perspectives on female giftedness. *Mensa Research Journal, 37,* 5–16.

Mattlin, J. A., Wethington, E., & Kessler, R. C. (1990). Situational determinants of coping and coping effectiveness. *Journal of Health and Social Behavior, 31*(1), 103–122.

Miller, J. B. (1986). *Toward a new psychology of women* (2nd ed). Boston, MA: Beacon Press.

Miller, J. B. (1994). Women's psychological development: Connections, disconnections and violations. In M.B. Berger (Ed.), *Women beyond Freud: New concepts in feminine psychology* (pp. 79–97). New York: Brunner/Mazel Publishers.

Navan, J. L. (1994). A writers' collaborative: The effects of collaborative learning on perceived self-efficacy. *Proceedings of the 1994 Conference of the Ontario Educational Research Council.* Toronto, ON: Ontario Education Research Council.

Navan, J. L. (2002). Constructs of efficacy in gifted young women. *Academic Exchange Quarterly, 10*(1)

Noble, K. D. & Smyth, R. K. (1995). Keeping their talents alive: Young women's assessment of radical post-secondary acceleration. *Roeper Review, 18*, 49–53.

Noble, K. D., Subotnik, R. F., & Arnold, K. D. (1999). To thine own self be true: A new model of female talent development. *Gifted Child Quarterly, 43*(4), 140–149.

Patterson, J. L. & Kelleher, P. (2005*). Resilient school leaders: Strategies for turning adversity into achievement*. Alexandria, VA: ASCD.

Pipher, M. B. (1994). *Reviving Ophelia: Saving the selves of adolescent girls*. New York: Putnam.

Reis, S. M. (2002). Social and emotional issues faced by gifted girls in elementary and secondary school. *SENG Newsletter, 2*(3), 1–5. Retrieved May 5, 2007 from http://www.sengifted.org/articles_social/Reis_SocialAndEmotionalIssuesFacedByGiftedGirls.shtml.

Reis, S. M. & Callahan, C. M. (1996). My boyfriend, my girlfriend, or me: The dilemma of talented teenage girls. *Journal of Secondary Gifted Education, 7*, 434–446.

Reis, S. M., Callahan, C. M., & Goldsmith, D. (1994). Attitudes of adolescent gifted girls and boys toward education, achievement, and the future. *Gifted Education International, 9*, 144–151.

Roeper, A. (2000). Giftedness is heart and soul. *Gifted Education Communicator, 31*(4), 32–33, 56–58.

Roeper, A. & Higgins, A. (2007). *The "I" of the beholder: A guided journey to the essence of a child*. Scottsdale, AZ: Great Potential Press.

Sands, T. & Howard-Hamilton, M. (1995). Understanding depression among gifted adolescent females: Feminist therapy strategies. *Roeper Review, 17*, 192–195.

Silverman, L. (2005). *An overview of issues in assessing gifted children*. Retrieved February 12, 2007, from http://www.gifteddevelopment.com/PDF_files/Assessment%20of20%Gifted%20Children.pdf.

Sollberg, V. S., Good, G. E., Fischer, A. R., Brown, S. D., & Nord, D. (1995). Career decision-making and career search activities: Relative effects of career search self-efficacy and human agency. *Journal of Counseling Psychology, 42*, 448–455.

Sprinthall, R. C., Sprinthall, N. A. & Oja, S. N. (1998*). Education Psychology: A Developmental Approach*, (7th Ed.). Boston, MA: McGraw-Hill.

Stepien, W. J. & Gallagher, S. A. (1993). Problem-based learning: As authentic as it gets. *Educational Leadership, 50*(7), 25–28.

Strip, C., Swassing, R., & Kidder, R. (1991). Female adolescents counseling female adolescents: A first step in emotional crises intervention. *Roeper Review, 13*, 124–128.

Walker, B. A. & Mehr, N, (1992). *The Courage to achieve: Why America's brightest women struggle to fulfill their promise*. New York: Simon & Schuster.

Webb, J. T., Amend, E. R., Webb, N.D., Goerss, J., Beljan, P., & Olenchak, F. R. (2005). *Misdiagnosis and Dual Diagnoses of Gifted Children and Adults*. Scottsdale, AZ: Great Potential Press.

Index

CORWIN
PRESS

The Corwin Press logo—a raven striding across an open book—represents the union of courage and learning. Corwin Press is committed to improving education for all learners by publishing books and other professional development resources for those serving the field of PreK–12 education. By providing practical, hands-on materials, Corwin Press continues to carry out the promise of its motto: **"Helping Educators Do Their Work Better."**